"Where did you go?"
"Out"

"What did you do?"
"Nothing"

"Where did you go?"
"Out"
"What did you do?"
"Nothing"

ROBERT PAUL SMITH

Drawings by James J. Spanfeller

W · W · NORTON & COMPANY · INC · *New York*

For Monica

"Where did you go?"
"Out"

"What did you do?"
"Nothing"

THE thing is, I don't understand what kids do with themselves any more. I have two boys of my own, I live in a suburb where three out of three fathers are up to here with catching that commuting train and paying that mortgage and burning those leaves and shoveling that snow, and when all else is indefensible, say, "But it's a wonderful place to raise children." Spock and Gesell and others of that Ilg are the local deities, the school teachers speak of that little stinker from Croveny Road as "a real challenge," there are play groups and athletic supervisors and Little Leagues and classes in advanced finger painting and family counselors and child psychologists. Ladies who don't know *a posteriori* from *tertium quid* carry the words "sibling rivalry" in the pocketbooks of their minds as faithfully as their no-smear lipstick.

And yet—I was with a bunch of kids a week ago, ranging in age from ten to fourteen (to forty-one counting me) and since none of them seemed to know what to do for the next fifteen minutes I said to them, "How about a game of mumbly-peg?" And can you believe that not one of these little siblings knew spank the baby from Johnny jump the fence? All right, I thought, they don't know mumbly-peg, maybe they're territory players. One of them knew that game. As a matter of fact, he beat me at it, but I figure that was because it was his knife. The wrong kind. When we were kids, we had a scout knife, and for only one reason. Oh, I know it says in the catalogs that that blade is a leather punch, but on my block that narrow fluted blade was a mumbly-peg blade. In an emergency you could punch a hole in something with the blade —but with us it was a knee or a forehead, most often, when we were doing knees or heads in mumbly-peg. It was *called* a scout knife, but it *was* a mumbly-peg knife.

On my block, when I was a kid, there was a lot of loose talk being carried on above our heads about how a father was supposed to be a pal to his boy. This was just another of those stupid things that grownups said. It was our theory that the grownup was the natural enemy of the child, and if any father had come around being a pal to us we would have figured he was either a little dotty or a spy. What we learned we learned from another kid. I don't remember being taught how to play mumbly-peg. (I know, I know. In the books they write it "mumblety-peg," but we said, and it *was*, "mumbly-peg.") When you were a little kid, you stood around while a covey of ancients of nine or ten played mumbly-peg, shifting from foot to foot and wiping your nose on your sleeve and hitching up your knickerbockers, saying, "Lemme do it, aw come on, lemme have a turn," until one of them struck you in a soft spot and you went home to sit under the porch by yourself or found a smaller kid to torture, or loused up your sister's rope-skipping, or made a collection of small round stones. The small round stones were not *for* anything, it was just to have a collection of small round stones.

One day you said, "Lemme have a turn, lemme have a turn," and some soft-hearted older brother, never your own, said, "Go-wan, let the kid have a turn," and there, by all that was holy, you were playing mumbly-peg.

Well now, I taught those kids to play mumbly-peg, and for all I know, if I hadn't happened to be around that day, in another fifteen years they would have to start protecting mumbly-peg players like rosy spoonbills or the passenger pigeon—but why don't the kids teach the other kids to play mumbly-peg? What do these kids do with themselves all the time?

So far as I can find out, they don't play immies any more. I see in the newsreels every once in a while that they're

holding the national marble championships. What kind of
an insanity is this? In the first place, any kid on my block
who called an immie a marble would have been barred from
civilized intercourse for life. In the second place, who cares
who's marble champion of the *world?* The problem is,
who's the best immie shooter on the block. And in the
third place, they play some idiotic kind of marbles with
a ring drawn in paint, and I'll bet a hat the rules are written down in a book. On my block, the rules were written
down in kids. The rules were that as soon as the ground
got over being frozen, any right-minded kid on the way
home from school, or in recess, planted his left heel in the
ground at an angle of forty-five degrees and walked around
it with his right foot until there was a hole of a certain
size. You couldn't measure this hole. We all knew what
size the hole was supposed to be. I could go outside right
now and make a hole the right size. (I did. It's still the
same size. The size of an immie hole. And while I was outside I drew a line with the toe of my foot the proper distance from the hole. It's still the same distance. It isn't
something you measure in feet. It's the distance from the
immie hole that the line is supposed to be.) Then you
stood on the line and, to start, threw immies, underhand, at
the hole. There was a kid who moved from another town
who said this was "lagging" but we didn't pay much attention to him. There's a lot more to immies. There's fins (or
fens) and knucks down and whether it was fair to wiggle

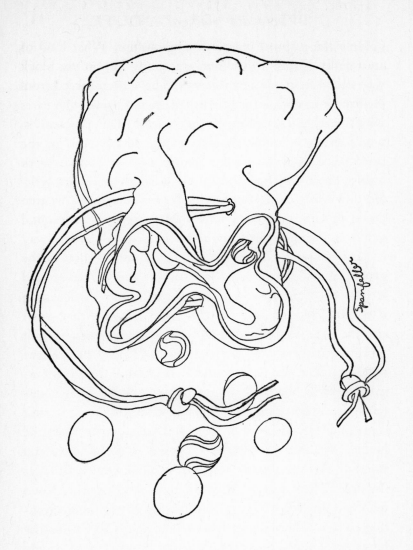

your feet while you were doing fins. (Or fens.) There were steelies, which were big ball bearings and could bust an immie and depending on the size of the kids these were legal or illegal, there were realies and glassies. There was the immie bag that your mother made and you put to one side because all right-minded kids carried them in a big bulge in the pocket until the pocket tore. The grownups used to talk about not playing for keeps, which was more nonsense like fathers being pals, and there was the time when I owed a boy I will call Charlie Pagliaro, because that was almost his name, one hundred and forty-four immies. He played me until I had no immies, then he extended me credit, and I doubled and redoubled, and staggered home trying to absorb the fact that I owed him one hundred and forty-four immies. Now the first thing to understand is that there is no such thing as one hundred and forty-four immies. Twenty maybe, or with the help of your good friends, thirty-six, or maybe by going into servitude for the rest of your life to every kid on the whole block, you might get up to about sixty. But there is no such thing as one hundred and forty-four marbles, that's the first thing. The second thing is that Charlie told me he would cut my head off with his knife—which was no boy scout knife, Charlie being, believe me, no boy scout. The third thing is that I believed Charlie would do it. The fourth thing is that I believed Charlie believed he would do it. I still do. Immies were a penny apiece then.

You go to your mother and say, "I owe Charlie Pagliaro one hundred and forty-four marbles." Your mother says, "I told you not to play for keeps." You go to your father and you say, "I owe Charlie Pagliaro one hundred and forty-four marbles." Your father says, "One hundred and forty-four? Well, tell him you didn't mean to go that high."

You go to your best friend. He believes that Charlie Pagliaro will cut your head off. He lends you three immies and a steelie, which, if I remember, was worth five immies, or if big enough, ten, if the guy you were swapping with wanted a steelie at all. Two copies of *The Boy Allies* and a box of blank cartridges, a seebackroscope you got from the Johnson Smith catalog, and a promise to Charlie Pagliaro that you will do his homework for the rest of your life, twenty-five cents in cash, and that's it. Charlie takes the stuff, and all you owe him now is fifteen immies. He knows you have a realie. Realies are worth more than diamonds. It is not a good thing to have Charlie mad at you. There goes the realie. You are alive, but poverty-stricken for all time.

(It occurs to me that Charlie Pagliaro may still be alive, and a pillar of the community. It occurs to me maybe you think of him as one of these kids you see around now, with those black leather jackets and motorcycle boots. That's wrong. I would be lying if I didn't say that he was tough. I would be lying if I didn't say that from time to time all of us kids threw rocks at each other, with the avowed intention of killing the other kid dead. I was no pillar of strength, and if it was possible to avoid having a fight with another kid, *any* other kid, I did. And even then, I had more than my share of fights. We fought and we stole and we lied and defended our honor and we lived by a code that had very little to do with an organization more high-minded than the Mafia. But Charlie didn't pull a knife on me, I don't believe he ever pulled a knife on anybody, and all the time we were engaged in juvenile rape and pillage, I never saw a kid deliberately hit another kid with anything but his hands or feet. There were a few wild men, who, aroused into red fury, laid hold of a handy one-by-two and let go, but nobody ever armed themselves for combat. This seems to have changed.)

So, they don't play mumbly-peg and they don't play immies. And all you people who are going to tell me about aggies, and the way you played marbles—peace. You played a different way. But whatever way you played, *that* was the way, that was the only way to play, and you would have had no more of me telling you then than I will of you telling me now. Most of all, did you ever in your whole life conceive of a grownup coming around and having the effrontery to butt into a game? It wasn't only that he would be silly, he wouldn't know. Also it was none of his goddam business. Oh, somebody's big brother, somebody who had used to be around the block, maybe even was going to college—*he* knew. We used to play football.

"Where did you go?" "OUT."

Nobody ever taught us, we played, and if somebody's big brother taught you the center was supposed (or not supposed?) to lean on the ball, that you had to get your fingers onto the seam to throw what we called "a sparrow," that was all right. He was a big kid. He wasn't a grownup. He was on our side.

I remember a baseball called a nickel rocket. I have a feeling even then inflation was on us and a nickel rocket cost ten cents. The first thing you did with a nickel rocket was to nip into somebody's garage and hook a roll of friction tape. If the garage was dark enough, for a minute or an hour you would grab the end of the tape and pull it back quickly and see the blue sparks. None of my teachers told me about static electricity, nor did anyone's father. I don't even know that they knew about this, or indeed that anybody but me knows about it to this day. Some kid found out that if you pulled the end of the tape back quickly, you saw blue sparks. Some kid told some other kid, and some other kid told some other kid. We knew it. All kids knew it. When we got tired of watching the sparks we wrapped the nickel rocket with friction tape, and if any was left over, we wrapped the handle of the bat with it. I guess I know now the reason we did this with the nickel rocket was that if by any wild chance one of us had gotten a solid hit, the ball would have come apart. But that's not the point. There was no reasoning going on then. You wrapped a nickel rocket with friction tape because that's what you

(16)

did with a nickel rocket. And you put it on the handle of the bat because there was some tape left over. And if there was still some left over, you put it around your wrist, like a strong man. And I have never thought about it until this minute, but why did people keep rolls of friction tape in the garage? We didn't know. It's just that that's where friction tape was. I feel it's got some connection with automobiles, that it was a way of helping to patch inner tubes, but I wouldn't bet a nickel either way.

There must have been some time in my life when I played baseball with nine men on a team, but surely it was not on our block. We played with as many kids as were around, and I don't think there were eighteen kids on the block. We always carefully looked at the bat to make sure the label was up, because if the label wasn't up, it would split the bat. Is there any truth in this? I don't know. It was an article of faith, and any kid who didn't turn the label up was screamed at until he did.

My kids don't play baseball because of their magnificent inheritance (constitutional sloth and an inability to get out of the way of their own feet), but all the kids I see playing baseball these days are in something called The Little League and have a covey of overseeing grownups hanging around and bothering them and putting catcher's masks on them and making it so bloody important the kids don't even know about one o' cat, or one old cat, or whatever you called it. They tell me these kids in the Little League cry

when they lose a game. Nobody ever cried in our baseball
games unless he caught a foul tip with the end of his finger,
or unless someone slang the bat and caught the catcher
across the shins with it, and since it was a kid umpiring, no
matter what the score came up finally, you could argue long
enough about any decision so that you either won or were
robbed. Or some kid had to leave in the middle to practice
the piano or go down to the store or go for a ride in his
uncle's new Essex. So, even though we never played nine
men on a side, nor were ever in a game that went nine
innings, what I remember is the sound of a ball in a glove,
and the feeling in my fingers when the bat threatened to
split (you vibrated clear up to your ears, and somebody
hollered at you to hold the label up) and I remember how
somebody got some very precious stuff called neat's-foot
oil ("It comes from the foot of a neat, you dope!") and
we rubbed that in our gloves instead of Three-in-One. And
then there was the little kid who had been given a glove
that we thought was much too good for him, and from the
loftiness of our advanced years, we advised him that the
only way to really truly properly break it in was to rub it
with horse dung and leave it in the sun.

Kids, as far as I can tell, don't do things like that any
more. There's always some interfering grownup around
being a pal to them, telling them where to put their feet
when they stand at the plate. We found out. Stand the way
you wanted to and there was everybody on your side

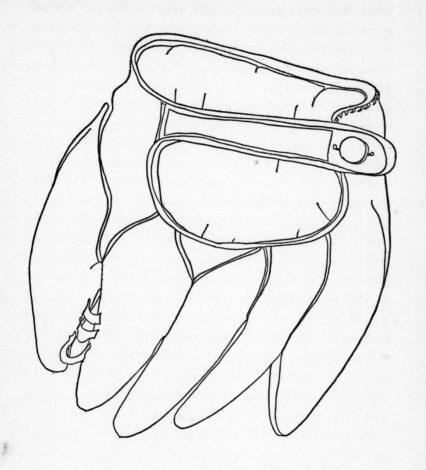

hollering "Take your foot out of the bucket," and you took your foot out of the bucket. When things got tough for our side, we picked out a real little kid, just big enough to hold the bat and stand at the plate. Just stand there, we told him, and the pitcher would carry on for a while, how it was gypping, who could throw strikes that low, then he'd throw him four straight balls and we had a man—a man!—on base.

Oh, all the wisdom. A kid hit a bunch of fouls. We knew what to say. "He's gonna have chicken for supper." Somebody was between you and what you wanted to see. "Sit down," we'd say, "waddya think, your father's a glazier?" We had, by the way, no idea of what a glazier was. Two infants would be flailing each other at recess, striking out like windmills and crying bitterly from pure rage. "Hit 'im in the kishkas," we said, "hit 'im in the bread basket, down in the la bonza, he don't like it down there."

We used to play a game called stoop ball. It is my considered reflection that for three months out of every year, for years on end, all we did was play stoop ball. It had to be played with a golf ball, I don't know why. After a certain amount of time, the golf ball—which we wouldn't have had at all unless the cover was cut almost to ribbons—would have enough cuts in it so you could pull off the white covering. Then for another three days, what you did was unwind the rubber band. I am not sure what you did with the rubber string you unwound, except to wrap it around various parts of your body until the circulation stopped. Mostly, once again, it was just what kids did. Unwound the rubber. In the center was a little white ball the size of an immie. Inside it, we knew, was something which was so dangerous it was inconceivable. There were two schools of thought. One, that it was an explosive so powerful that, that, that—well jeez, it was an *explosive!* The other school of thought held that it was a poison that killed, not only on contact anybody who was foolhardy enough to open it, but it would strike dead, on the whole block, every person, cat, collie dog. It could also wither trees and probably melt the pavement.

We cut one open once, and a thick white liquid dribbled out. I was the wise guy. Somebody said it was poison, so I had to say it wasn't. I touched it. Catch me doing that today! That stuff there, that stuff—why jeez, it's an explosive!

I suppose this is all just an indication of my advanced years, but I don't know things now like I used to know then. What we knew as kids, what we learned from other kids, was not tentatively true, or extremely probable, or proven by science or polls or surveys. It was so. I suppose this has to do with ontogeny recapitulating phylogeny. We were savages, we were in that stage of the world's history when the earth stood still and everything else moved. I wrote on the flyleaf of my schoolbooks, and apparently every other kid in the world did, including James Joyce and Abe Lincoln and I am sure Tito and Fats Waller and Michelangelo, in descending order my name, my street, my town, my county, my state, my country, my continent, my hemisphere, my planet, my solar system. And let nobody dissemble: it started out with me, the universe was the outer circle of a number of concentric rings, and the center point was me, me, me, sixty-two pounds wringing wet with heavy shoes on. I have the notion, and perhaps I am wrong, that kids don't feel that way any more. Damn Captain Video! And also, I am afraid, damn "The Real True Honest-to-God Book of Elementary Astrophysics in Words of One Syllable for Pre-School Use."

Once again, it's because we grownups are always around pumping our kids full of what we laughingly call facts. They don't want science. They want magic. They don't want hypotheses, they want immutable truth. They want to be, they should be, in a clearing in the jungle painting themselves blue, dancing around the fire and making it rain by patting snakes and shaking rattles. It is so strange: nobody, so far as I know, sat around worrying about the insides of our heads, and we made ourselves safe. Time enough to find out, as we are finding out now, that nothing is so. Not even close to so.

But then: facts, facts, facts. If you cut yourself in the web of skin between your thumb and forefinger, you die. That's it. No ifs or buts. Cut. Die. Let's get on to other things. If you eat sugar lumps, you get worms. If you cut a worm in half, he don't feel a thing, and you get two worms. Grasshoppers spit tobacco. Step on a crack, break your mother's back. Walk past a house with a quarantine sign, and don't hold your breath, and you get sick and die. Play with yourself too much, your brain gets soft. Cigarettes stunt your growth. Some people are double-jointed, and by that we didn't mean any jazz like very loose tendons or whatever the facts are. This guy had two joints where we had one. A Dodge (if your family happened to own a Dodge) was the best car in the whole world.

We cut our fingers in that web and didn't die, but our convictions didn't change. We ate sugar lumps, and I don't recall getting worms, but the fact was still there. We'd pass by the next day and both halves of the worm would be dead, our mother's back never broke, my sister had scarlet fever right in my own house and I must have breathed once or twice in all that time, none of our brains got *real* soft, and we really knew that what came out of the grasshopper was not tobacco juice. But facts were one thing, and beliefs were another.

We got our schoolbooks, and we went home and in a drawer in the kitchen was a pile of wrapping paper saved from packages, and we folded covers for the books in a certain way. Some kids came to our town from New York City, and they told us that you could go to a stationery store in New York and *buy* covers for schoolbooks, but we got them over lying like that. Some of the girls used wallpaper for their covers, and some of them used glue for the folded-over flaps, but they were wrong. Even they knew that. The right way was to fold it. The drawer with the wrapping paper was the drawer with the string. We were rich. We could have had a ball of string if we wanted one, I guess. But we didn't, and nobody I knew did. We had pieces of string. To this day I cannot understand why, right now in my own house, we don't have a drawer with pieces of wrapping paper and pieces of string. My wife, who grew up in New York, *buys* wrapping paper and throws pieces of string away. She doesn't save boxes, either, or empty spools, and she doesn't have a button box. She says that packages largely do not come wrapped in wrapping paper any more, and if they do they are sealed down with tape, and you have to tear the paper to get it off, and I guess she's right about that, and I suppose there's nothing really immoral about springing ten cents for a ball of twine, and our kids wear Tee shirts and pants with zippers on them, so where the hell are the buttons going to come from, but that's all in the realm of reason and you know what kind of sense women make when it comes to reason. She doesn't even rub the cut-off tip of a cucumber against the rest of it to draw the poison out. *She* doesn't even think there's anything wrong with the kids eating pickles and milk at the same meal. Not that they get sick from it, not that I really think they're going to—but she isn't even scared. Why, I tell you about this woman—she thinks it's all right to go to the movies in the afternoon, and sleep with the windows closed, and once she let the kids have candy before lunch.

My little boy was mooning around the house the other day—it is one of the joys of being a writer that occasionally when *I* am mooning around the house because I haven't the vaguest idea of what to do about the second act, or the last chapter, or Life, or why I don't have an independent income or a liquor store or a real skill like a tool-and-die maker or a lepidopterist or a mellophone player—I can slope downstairs and trap a child. The littler boy was mooning around. I was mooning around. He had no idea what to do with himself because his room is full of wood-burning kits and model ships to be made out of plastic and phonographs and looms and Captain Kangaroo Playtime Kits and giant balloons and plaster of paris and colored pencils and compasses and comic books and money. I will straighten this little bugger out, I said, I will pass on to him the ancient knowledge of his sire, I will teach him a little something about the collective unconscious, by God I will. "Did you ever make a buzz-saw out of a button?" I opened brightly. He thought for a while, and tried to remember what a button was, and concluded that it was something like a zipper, but he didn't know what a buzz-saw was. He decided that a buzz-saw was like what I almost cut my thumb off with in the cellar and had out of the house by nightfall. "First thing we need is a big button," I said, and

"*What did you do?*" "NOTHING."

then we went into that thing about, "I don't know where there's a button, for the love of God ask your mother, of course there's a button around the house. Where? In the button box."

That's when I found out we don't have a button box. We went to our neighbor's and after a while they found a button box. Not their button box, but one that Grandma had had. We got a big button. I strung it with a loop of silk thread, and it didn't work and the thread broke. I suppose nobody bothers making silk thread strong now, if you want strong thread you use nylon. When I was a kid, silk thread was so strong you practically cut the tip of your finger off breaking it. *That* was thread. We went to look for string, but all there was was a ball of very good string that was too thick. We went back to the neighbor with the button box and in *her* kitchen drawer there was an assortment of bits of string. We made a buzz-saw. He took it to day camp with him. The other kids thought it was a new kind of yo-yo and wanted to know where to buy one. When my kid told them his father had made it, they decided he was a liar.

On Sunday I went over to another neighbor. He had called me because he couldn't stand it around his house any more and wanted to come to my house, but I thought fast and said I'd be over to his house because (I didn't tell him this) I couldn't stand my house any more. You know, of course, that visiting in the suburbs is not so much a journey to a friend as a flight from an enemy: home. You sit around a friend's house and after a couple of hours you are so pleased to discover that your kids don't spit up their bottles any more—as well they might not at eight and ten—so delighted that your wife doesn't even try to make you clip the hedge any more, that it's going to cost him three times as much to put a new roof on as it's going to cost you to have the porch shored up (neither of you can afford to do either), that his wife has some sort of jackass notion that men are supposed to shave and mix daiquiris for people— well, I tell you, it's nice to get home.

But this day I thought if I had to watch my wife do one more puzzle in the Sunday paper—she does the crossword, the diagramless crossword, the crosswordless diagram, the cryptogram, the double-crostic, the triple-crostic with a one and a half gainer—if I had to listen to one more of those puny ideas from the littler boy—the older is away at camp and I am spared disquisitions about "Isn't it interesting that Jupiter has three freeble-tropic moons that travel in an elliptical granster with a mean clyde-bender ratio of . . ." —but the littler boy has problems like, "My counselor said he had a pet mouse and he fed him every day and the mouse got bigger and bigger and one day he exploded, do you believe that's true, well if it was a joke why wasn't he smiling when he told me about it?" Another fifteen minutes of this and the inside of my head telling me in louder and louder tones, "You haven't written a line in two weeks, you're getting older and you haven't got a dime in the bank, and if you don't finish the play—maybe you aren't a writer at all. After all, you could go to an office and there would be a pile of papers on one side of the desk in the in-basket and at the end of the day you could have moved them all to the other side of the desk to the out-basket and have two weeks' vacation with pay, and if you can't write for two weeks, chances are you'll never write another line as long as you live, and if you do nobody will publish it or produce it or—and drinking isn't so much fun any more and she's going to keep on with those goddam puzzles, she doesn't care, and how the hell do I know. Maybe there is a disease that makes mice explode, and look at that porch, it's going to fall down any minute."

Well, you go over to visit a neighbor. Oh, if he could only get away from that desk and those in-baskets and out-baskets, what's it like to be a free lance, you make a lot of money and you have your time to yourself and you meet glamorous people, and one of his kids is lying belly-down on the dining room table saying, "Moooo . . . moooo . . . oh, mooo." Papa has some gin and you have some gin, and after a while, another of his kids slopes in and before you know it, you say, "Did you ever make a spool tank?"

He doesn't know any more about a spool tank than your flesh and blood knew about a buzz saw. You need a spool, a rubber band, a candle and two kitchen matches, you tell him, confident that none of these things will be available.

You have a little more gin. He turns up with a rubber band, a candle, and two kitchen matches. He asks his mother for a spool. He comes back with a spool that has at least three feet of thread left on it. You relax, and *this* mother, this flouter of tradition, *goes ahead and tells this kid he can unwind and throw away the three feet of thread.* When we were kids, we had to wait at least six months for an empty spool. A spool was empty when the thread was used up. For sewing. There was one big spool in my mother's sewing box, the kind that they use in factory sewing machines. It would have made a spool tank bigger than any on the block. On the block hell, in the world. It would have used rubber bands cut from an inner tube and a wax washer cut from a plumber's candle and pencils instead of matches. I wanted that spool more than I have wanted anything else in my life until I was fifteen and saw Mary Astor. I'm still waiting for it. It had thread on it, and when the world was running right, kids who wanted spools had to wait for empty spools.

The thing that bothered me about the spool tank I made the other day (it ran magnificently, as always, and I expect some shrewd fellow is going to bring out a goddam kit for kids to make them, with a plastic spool and a fiberglas washer and a super-latex band), the thing that bothered me is I think I made it at the wrong time. I don't think it was the spool tank season.

You see, when I was a kid, the year was divided into

times. There was a time when you played immies. There was a time when you played stoop ball. There was a time when you built kites. There was a time when you made parachutes out of a handkerchief and some string and a rock. There was a time when you made spool tanks. There was a time when you played football. There was a time when you played Red Rover, and statues, and one and over and Buck Billy Buck and ringeleveo. Everybody did it. It was like the trees coming into green. There was something that clicked, and the gears shifted, and we all got up in the morning and put our immies in our pockets because that was the day everybody started to play immies. And when the immie season was over, we all knew it. We didn't even talk about it. It was just the end of the immie season, and one morning we stopped playing immies and started making kites, because overnight it had stopped being immie time and started being kite time.

There were other divisions: up until, say seven, boys could play hopscotch. Then, the iron door slammed. From there on out, hopscotch was for girls. On my block, no boy could ever, at whatever age, skip rope. Once in a while, a boy could play higher and higher, which was simply two girls holding the skipping rope (a piece of clothesline, and I'll get into that later) higher and higher while a boy jumped until he got his foot caught in the rope and fell on his face. Girls could ride boys' bikes, but boys couldn't ride girls' bikes. Girls could play tag, but not leapfrog. (My, we were backward children.) Girls could carry their books in both arms across their bellies, but boys had to carry them in one hand against their sides. Girls could play immies, occasionally, under great conditions of tolerance, but not mumbly-peg—until around fourteen, when boys would let girls do anything, having plans for later that night, under the street lamps.

That's another thing. Now it is summer, in this perishing suburb where I live, to which we moved because when we lived in the city, we had to go away every summer so the kids could learn about grass. There are the long evenings, and you can hear what the neighbors are saying, and the other night we went out in the back yard to lie on our backs on a blanket and watch the meteor showers, and there is the big problem of the gardeners who overinvested in tomato plants (for years the littler boy could not be talked out of his belief in elves, because mysterious figures appeared in the night and left boxes of tomatoes at the back door) and dogs would be lying in the middle of the road with their tongues lolling out except there is a law saying they must be leashed until five o'clock, so they loll leashed, and cats hide in the weed jungles, and we see baby rabbits caught in the headlight glare, and the neighbor for whose son I built a spool tank came around with a day-lily the size of my head that smells like a sixteen year old girl (not the lady or my head, but the lily). And the town is a tomb. There are no kids, the Pied Piper has been by.

"*What did you do?*" "NOTHING."

It is summer, and there are the long evenings under the street lamps to talk to girls, to watch the big kids talking to girls, to tease the big kids talking to girls, to be hit by the big kids talking to girls, to play Red Rover, to sit on the porch steps and listen to your father tell Mister Fenyvessey what he thinks of the Republicans, to tell your best friend what your father told Mister Fenyvessey and what Mister Fenyvessey told your father, and what words your father used. It is summer and it is time to get a jelly glass and fill it full of lightning bugs and tie a piece of gauze over the top and take it to your room, and very late at night to see that your finger, where you touched the lightning bug, is glowing too.

But not in our town. The kids are at camp, because, for Heaven's sake, what are the kids going to do with themselves all summer? Well, it would be nice, I think, if they spent an afternoon kicking a can. It might be a good thing if they dug a hole. No, no, no. Not a foundation, or a well, or a mother symbol. Just a hole. For no reason. Just to dig a hole. After a while, they could fill it with water, if they liked. They might find a stone that they could believe was an axe-head, or a fossil. They might find a penny. Or a very antique nail. Or a bone. A saber-tooth tiger's kneecap. Or if they didn't want to fill the hole with water, they could put something in it like a penny, or a nail, or an axe-head, or a dead bird and cover it with dirt and leave it there for a while, so they could dig it up later and see what happens

(33)

to something that you leave in the dirt for a while. We usually forgot to dig it up, or forgot where we had buried it, but once it was a turtle which had made itself dead, and when we dug it up, some obliging beetles had eaten it clean, and I had an empty turtle shell, and that was a good thing to have.

About the Red Rover. We used to use the names of cars. And if it was a hot evening and you didn't want to run, you picked out an obscure name like Simplex, and to this day I can hear the calls in the summer evening under the street lamp. "Pierce Arrow, come over. Hupmobile, come over. Locomobile, come over. Stanley Steamer, Kissel, Moon, Essex, come over. Go-wan, there's no such a car as a Buckboard. Is there, Piggy, is there. It's a kind of a car, not a make of a car, it's like saying, Coupe (and that was coo-pay) come over. Mercedes-Benz, come over. Hispano-Suiza, come over. Isotta-Fraschini, come over." Oh, we were a cosmopolitan crowd.

The kids could have watered the lawn in the summer. I could have watered them when I watered the lawn. When I was a kid, you watered the lawn by standing there and holding the hose and spraying it back and forth. In arcs, and in fountains, and in figure eights, and straight up in the air, energetically, and dreamily and absentmindedly, washing the walk, and the porch and the window screen and your father in the living room reading the paper. You dug trenches with the stream from the hose and filled milk bot-

(34)

tles and garbage cans and the back seats of parked cars. And
if it was a grownup watering the lawn, you hung around
until he said, "Why don't you kids go ask your mothers if
you can get in your bathing suits and I'll spray you," and
you pounded home and got into the scratchy wool bathing
suit and pounded back and there, I tell you, was Heaven on
earth, getting wet on a front lawn on purpose.

But now we have sprinklers that are scientific and you
can sit indoors watching some people play Red Rover on
television while your sprinkler crawls along its hose, spraying a predetermined pattern.

It was a hot day, and the clouds gathered and the rain
came, the heavy heavy fat drops of summer making quar-
ters on the sidewalk, and in every house screen doors
slammed, and it was, "Mother, mother, can I," and all over
the block kids ran out, in their scratchy woolen bathing
suits, dancing up and down in the rain. The kids could have
done that in the summer.

They could have found their best friend and gone for a
long walk, kicking a can, and after a while, lying on their
backs against a hedge somewhere, looking up in the sky
and speculating. They could have done the same thing,
alone, in the back yard, seeing the shapes swimming in the
sky. I forget how old I was when I asked somebody about
it, and I was told that those wonderful gliding changing
spots were imperfections in the fluid of my eye-ball, that
what I was seeing was in my eye. In *your* eye! For so long,

for a child's years, the sky was full of wonder, these shapes were in the sky, the sky was full of transparent things that swooped and swam. They were almost invisible, and, I thought, almost bodiless, they were there, but you could go right through them, they were animals that lived in the air. You see, we didn't go around talking about things like this. It's only now, that I am grown up and know everything, that I talk about this.

LYING awake at night, knuckling my eyeballs so that I could see the flashes of light, the fireworks that only I knew about. Taking off the rubber band that I had wrapped around my thumb, tight, so that I could feel the prickles, the electricity, the exquisite torture of the slow removal of the garter. Going to sleep with my right big toe in my left hand, my right arm wrapped around my head holding the lobe of my left ear, to find out if I would wake up that way in the morning. Sitting on the back steps with my friend and a milk bottle, putting in a piece of licorice, and some medicine he had found when his mother cleaned out the medicine chest, and some salt and some pepper and a bit of chocolate, some raspberry jam and a piece of iron, a little ketchup and a rubber band, water and milk and a little square of water-color paint prized out of my sister's paintbox. Shaking it up and wishing we had something to make it fizz, and daring each other to drink it, and tasting it, and saying it's good, it really is *good*.

You see, it never occurred to us that there was anything wrong in doing nothing, so long as we kept out of the way of grownups. These days, you see a kid lying on his back and looking blank and you begin to wonder what's wrong with him. There's nothing wrong with him, except he's thinking. He's trying to find out whether he breathes differently when he's thinking about it than when he's just breathing. He's seeing how long he can sit there without blinking. He is considering whether his father is meaner than Carl's father, he is wondering who he would be if his father hadn't married his mother, whether there is somewhere in the world somebody who is exactly like him in every detail up to and including the fact that the other one is sitting there thinking whether there is someone who is exactly like him in every detail. He is trying to arrive at some conclusion about his thumb.

But when we were kids, we had the sense to keep these things to ourselves. We didn't go around asking grownups about them. They obviously didn't know. We asked other kids. They knew. I think we were right about grownups being the natural enemies of kids, because we knew that what they wanted us to do was to be like them. And that was for the birds. "Pop, look at this. It's a pollywog, look at it." "Um," said your father. Another kid said, "Jeez, where'd you get it? Are there any more? What'll you take for it?"

"Hey, mother, you know what? Ted Fenster's kid brother eats dirt." "Well, don't let me catch you doing it," said your mother. "Go-wan," a kid would say. "Eats dirt? You mean, really eats dirt? Yer full of it." "He'll do it for a penny," you said, and you went off to find Ted Fenster's kid brother, and by God, he ate dirt, lots of it, spoonfuls of it, for a penny.

My kids have got a phonograph that plays three speeds, and the amount of antiseptic garbage that comes in three speeds these days about woolly bears, and floppy rabbits and Zoo-zoo the Xylophone and Serpentine the Slide Trombone is having only one effect. They don't play the phonograph very much, and when they do, they play 33's at 45, or 45's at 78, they endeavor to play them backward and sideways—anything at all in an attempt to have something to *do* with the phonograph. When I was a kid, we had one, God save the mark, "kiddie" record, a small disk on which a remote baritone sang "Fiddle Dee Dee, Fiddle Dee Dee, the fly has married the bumble bee," and let me assure you, he was not singing it so kids could understand it, or sing with it, or learn the happy playtime customs of foreign lands. He was standing up in front of a mike and belting it out like a proper singer. When I was old enough to make my wants known, that record was retired. It occurs to me that it never occurred to me that there was anything to be comprehended about this record, bar the song. I never was told, nor would I have listened if anyone had tried to tell me, that there was any meaning to it. Who the fly was, or why he wanted to marry the bumble bee, or indeed when I first heard it, *what* a fly, a bumble bee, or marrying meant, was something beyond my ken. But I can still remember the words, more or less, and the tune, and what the man's voice sounded like, and what the record looked like—it was small, like a 45 record today, it had a white label with some birds on it. As I say, that one went on the retired list as soon as I learned to crank the phonograph. I learned to crank it shortly after I discovered, by looking, that grownups had lied to me when they told me there was a little man sitting inside the machine and singing. By the way, I didn't feel betrayed that they had lied to me. Of course grownups didn't tell the truth. That was article one.

Once I learned to crank it, I also learned that if I didn't crank it enough, it would run down. And oh, the pure joy of listening to Caruso turn from a tenor into a bass! Oh, the sheer delight of having every grownup within hearing distance turn purple at hearing the Victor Salon orchestra in a medley of songs from "The Bohemian Girl" turn into a combination German band, barnyard, slide whistle, and bass fiddle choir, and then, by judicious cranking, hear it turn back into music again. You could also put things on

the turntable, pencils, marbles, pieces of chalk, horse chestnuts, and see how long it would take for them to fly off the
turntable and how far under the couch they would go. No
jolly little round songs about the friendly little mongoose
going buckety-buckety down the big big road with all his
woolly little woodland friends to the neurotic old tiger's
house. Cohen on the Telephone, and Harry Lauder, Moran
and Mack, John McCormack, and one record by I know
not who, of "Kol Nidre" that chilled me to the marrow.
Belle Baker, Bert Williams, Martinelli, Galli Curci (surely
then the funniest name for the funniest voice in the world),
and Caruso, Caruso, Caruso, and to this day, I, the musical
idiot, the opera-hater, go soft all over when I hear the aria
from *The Pearl Fishers.*

I have a feeling that there was one record that was called,
simply, "Barnyard Sounds" and was, simply, barnyard
sounds, possibly a man imitating barnyard sounds, perhaps
a real honest bunch of chickens and ducks and donkeys
making a day's pay. And I think another, a cello solo, and
later on, when my sisters started to dance—but that was a
different world, and, I am certain, a different phonograph.
The records, you remember, were black, and they had black
labels, didn't they, with gold type? They were easily a
quarter of an inch thick, and most of them had grooves on
one side only. They were to records today as a linen handkerchief is to a Kleenex. These things, too, you see, were
not tentative, not provisional. These records were.

(45)

I learned that I did not like singing, very much. I learned that when the records went around slow, the sounds were low, when they went around fast, the sounds were high. This, I believe, is science, and I found it out for myself. I found out that when the turntable went around fast, the horse chestnut flew off. I would like to say that I found out that heavy things flew off faster than light things, but I don't know if that's true. I think it's true. I think that's what I later learned was called centrifugal force. But right this minute, if I want to know about centrifugal force, I have to think about that turntable, I can see it all right, and of course, I can see it clearly, the marble went off before the chalk, not because it was round, I don't think, but because it was heavier. I have recently inquired, and have been told, that things fly off a rotating disc according to the relation between their coefficient of weight and their coefficient of friction, or something like that. Well, if you want to believe that kind of talk . . . All I know is, the marble landed under the couch, just this minute, and my head was over to one side and I saw the big iron lamp standard, the Chinese one with the dragons crawling all over it, and overhead the big beautiful yellow silk shade with the fringe that I could not keep from unraveling, the heavy cord that switched the lights on and off. I remember the heavy cord because it had some sort of weight on the bottom, maybe another piece of iron with a dragon on it. In any event, it was a very comforting thing to pop in and out of my mouth. It made a noise, and it was cool.

The fire tools were kind of nice. There was a poker and a shovel and a pincers that made, by itself, a satisfactory noise when clicked, and even more when applied to a re- cumbent sister's bottom. That noise was followed imme- diately by the noise of the whole rack clattering to the floor, sometimes the fire screen as well, the front door slamming, and my sister's voice through the door promising imminent and total destruction as soon as I let go the door knob on my side of the front door, and then, of course, the tiresome intervention of a parent. On my sister's side, of course.

I didn't get licked, nor did my sisters. How they felt about it, I don't know, but I remember kids coming to school and telling with pride of the licking their father had given them. Peace, peace, truculent reader—I am not saying anything one way or the other about corporal punishment. I think it's a hell of a note for somebody six feet tall to beat up on somebody two or three or four feet tall. But it does give the four-footer a clear idea of the way things are, be- cause whether by belt or hand or moral persuasion, the kid knows the six-footer is going to have his way. And when these kids came to school and told about the licking they had gotten, all of us un-licked kids knew that these kids had reached freedom. The enemy had shown his hand, and they weren't confused about why the parent was right. He was right because he had the might, and the thing to do was get mighty, and then let's see who's boss. In the meantime, lay low, and don't give any secrets away. And don't for a moment think that we, as kids, didn't know that the parent had lost when he gave you a licking, and felt terrible about it, and could be angled and played and hooked and landed. It's a funny thing, but my impression is that it was always the kids who got the lickings who got the bee-bee guns. I suppose, even in our middle-class community, there were parents who got their kicks out of beating up their kids, but I don't suppose that has changed any. I do know that one day, walking with my mother, she saw a mother slapping a child, and without a moment's hesitation, walked over to this total stranger and told her to stop, and the other mother stopped. Of course, I got jawed and shamed, and black-mailed and cried over and despaired of, and would have been charmed to swap all that in on one good brief physical interlude, but then . . .

I only got spanked once. My sister was lying on the floor. She was lying on the floor, reading the funny papers on a Sunday morning. (That, thank the Lord, hasn't changed. My kids belly down on the living-room floor for the same reason. I have hope for them.) I was walking around, and at this moment I'd give eight to five I was walking around trying to find someone to read the funny papers to me. I'd give two to one I was counting on the younger of my two older sisters to read them to me. She was easier to cajole than the other. In any event, I stepped on her hand, and she said ouch. My father spanked me, not because I stepped on her hand, but because I wouldn't apologize. I wouldn't apologize because I had myself convinced that I had not done it on purpose. And maybe I hadn't. Now this was a defense in those days. You had to apologize if you did it on purpose, and you did not have to apologize if it was an accident, and it was incumbent on the honor of the individual kid to say whether it was on purpose or an accident. In direct violation of this eternal provision of The Law, my father took out and spanked me. It then became, in my mind, a moral issue. I had very little hesitation in lying from then on. I stayed out of my father's way, too, which wasn't hard, because he stayed out of the way of all of us as much as he could. And since he was sick, that was a lot. But all of the fathers stayed away from the little kids. Mothers took care of little kids. Fathers read their papers and smoked their cigars and went for walks and played pinochle and golf. My father, I was told, once took me out in my baby-carriage, he pushed it himself, and it was enough to mark him an odd one for months.

But he licked me, that once, and I bawled, and I knew who he was from then on. He was the one who didn't obey The Law.

It is curious, but the way I learned about stealing was the same sort of thing. In my day, there were established orders of punishment in school. First, there was staying after school. Second, there was being sent to the cloakroom. Third, there was being sent to the principal's office. Fourth was the summoning of parents. Fifth, there was being—well, I don't know the word. It was a public school, so I suppose you couldn't have been expelled. But whatever it was called, it meant that you could not come to school unless something or other was done. You couldn't stay home either, because your parents wouldn't have it. It was for a major crime, and I suppose the nearest thing to it I ever ran across, except the thing itself, was Dante's limbo.

I was a good little boy. I was a smart little boy. I was a meek and well-behaved little boy. And yet, I experienced these punishments in all but the fourth degree. Because I was also a smart-aleck of a little boy.

First, we'll take the second, being sent to the cloakroom. Of course I was sent to the cloakroom unjustly. In all the history of the world, no teacher has ever sent the guilty party to the cloakroom. I mean, if the kid behind me goosed me under the seat, then I had to hit him, because when I had got him for two for biting in recess, there was a law saying you had to hit him in the muscle as hard as you could and he had no right to—well, you remember. So, I was sent to the cloakroom. In the cloakroom there was remarkably little to do. After a while, in the gloom at one end, I found a chalk box. I'll bet a hat chalk no longer comes in wooden boxes with sliding tops and a thumbnail slit, and wasn't it packed in sawdust too? (Nowadays it probably comes in plastic containers that dispense one stick at a time in a sanitary cellophane wrapper with pictures of rabbits on it.) In any event, there was a chalk box. That is to say, a box full of chalk. We would as lief gone out on the streets without our pants—no, that's a bad simile, that we would have been delighted to do—without, oh, a piece of string and an acorn and a shingle nail, and an empty aspirin bottle as without a piece of chalk. It was, yes it was, and yes, I did turn into a novelist, for writing dirty words, and arrows, and unkind comments about contemporaries on the sidewalk. I slid back the top of the box.

NOW HEAR THIS: There was no chalk in that box. It was full of knives. Why, it will appear presently.

When we appeared in school, we were frisked. We were searched for the carrying of concealed dirt under the nails; we were required to have, in lieu of an identification card, one clean handkerchief. I wonder, parenthetically, whether kids nowadays know the meaning of the phrase, "Is it for show or for blow?" This handkerchief was for show, it was a passport, and it didn't matter a great deal how grimy it was, by law it was clean if it was folded and unblown-in. If you didn't have a handkerchief in your pocket, you were sent off to the boy's room for a swatch of toilet paper. That was the days of highly varnished toilet paper, like the

English still use, and it was about as useful for blowing your nose in as for its avowed purpose. But no matter. It had nothing to do with blowing your nose. It was no more meant for function than any other legal document.

Now, that was what you had to have. If, in addition, you bore any livestock, wittingly or not, you were in the toils of authority. I, for one, fell madly in love with a little girl who came from the wrong side of the tracks because she smelled so wonderful. She smelled of kerosene. Our teacher, walking down the aisle, had run a pencil through her hair, as she did to all of us, why, I never knew. She had found something in Rose's hair, Rose had been packed off to the school nurse, Rose had come back smelling gloriously of kerosene. I loved the smell of kerosene. Rose smelled of kerosene. I loved Rose.

She was an involuntary smuggler, but others were criminals by volition and were dealt with in open court. Other livestock, such as caterpillars, large beetles, small toads, were, if detected, carried outside by you, deposited somewhere in the yard, and later on you were kept after school.

And now the knives: knives were confiscated, not to be returned, if they became visible during school hours. This was more of The Law. You could have a knife in your pocket. You could carry the knife to school in your pocket. You could keep your hand on your knife in your pocket during school. But if that hand came out of that pocket with that knife and was seen by your teacher, you were summonsed, you marched to the desk, you put the knife on the desk, and you never saw it again.

Until this day, in the cloakroom, when I opened the chalk box and found it full of knives, confiscated knives, knives seized without due process of law over the years from us second-class citizens.

I had a mother who had two daughters older than me, and a constant refrain of my childhood was, "Your sisters never asked for anything like that." This particular episode was when I was very young, and what I had been asking for, and had been refused, was a knife. I would like to tell you that I struggled with my conscience in the cloakroom, that I wrestled for my soul, and came out of the cloakroom a bigger and better and knifeless man. But in all truth, I must tell you I hooked a knife without a moment's hesitation, put it in my pocket with nothing but glee, and never in all of my forty-one conscience-ridden years have I ever felt one little twinge. The world owed me a knife and I took it.

I am a good father and a dutiful husband. I have been married for sixteen years. I have diapered the children, and physicked them, I have talked to them and listened to them, I have bathed them and rocked them to sleep, I have swum with them and piggybacked them and attended them in hospitals and restaurants and doctors' offices and airplanes and automobiles and I believe I know them very well. On the witness stand, ask me to swear what grade they are in, *for sure*, what is the color of their eyes, *absolutely*, what is the exact height of my wife, does she prefer rutabagas to Jerusalem artichokes, *under oath*—I don't know.

But if you would care to hear an exact description of that knife, I can go on for some time. It had two blades, and a horn handle, and brass bolsters and—but what's the use. They don't make that kind of knife any more. I know, because I have at home now, all told, about eight knives, the last bought within the year. I bought every one of them because it was close to that knife. But it's not the same.

So that's the moral lesson I learned from being sent to the cloakroom—unjustly. If they call you a criminal, for Heaven's sake, behave like one.

Now we go back to offenses punishable in the first degree: by being kept after school. What I learned from that was that, with my atrocious penmanship, the more times I wrote out, "I will never again . . ." the more illegible it got, and the more my fingers hurt, and the more I could swagger when I got back to the block and announced gruffly, "Old Piano Legs kept me in again." Moral: if you can't lick authority, give it a bad name.

About the Bringing of Parents to School, present deponent knoweth not.

Sometime in my early school years, the enlightened administration of the school decided not to grade kids on the basis of 100 on a report card, or even Excellent, Good, Fair, Poor. It was to be *tout court* Satisfactory or Unsatisfactory.

"What did you do?" "NOTHING."

I brought home report cards which were depressingly the
same. I was Satisfactory in all subjects but one. Month after
month, Penmanship, Unsatisfactory. My mother looked at
the report cards, adjured me to write better, signed them
and I brought them back. That was my parents' connection
with the school. By the way, the system broke down, in-
stanter. It was no time at all until we were off into Very
Satisfactory, Quite Satisfactory, Almost Unsatisfactory,
More or Less Totally Unsatisfactory and suchlike embroi-
dery. There was the usual Could Do Better If He Applied
Himself, or Is Making Satisfactory Progress. And once in a
while, Is Doing Very Well. But always, these were in a
grudging tone which, honestly, we liked. They were deco-
rations extorted from the enemy. There was no blarney like
I see on my kids' report cards, about real challenges, and
gets along well with the group, and does not (or does) par-
ticipate helpfully in social integration. We knew where we
stood. When we *made* a teacher confess that we were good,
by God, we were *good*. I don't think my kids can tell any
more whether anybody thinks they're making out: they're
being bathed in such a sweet syrup of reassurance that nothing short of a twenty-one-gun salute is going to convince
them that they've done anything extraordinarily good,
nothing but a jail term is going to convey disapproval. I
don't really think that: I think they know—as kids always
know—when somebody's conning them. *They* know, even
if we don't, whether they're cutting ice. But if they're will-

ing, and they are, to face a few facts, it seems to me shameful we're not willing to level with them.

Now, about punishment in the fifth degree. I don't know much about how it went with other kids, but the way it happened to me was the first time the public school system of my town was up against my peculiar brand of hard head. If you set fire to the school, my guess is you got expelled, and probably sent to reform school. If you had the colossal insanity to raise your hand to a teacher as far as we knew, you got killed. If you didn't study, you got left back—how many times you could get left back, I don't know.

But I was something new. I was the first rebel on literary principle. We had a teacher who was interested in teaching, and we loved her and crucified her daily by the clock. We talked about things, and read things, and it was this teacher who first pointed out to me a small defect in my character which certain malcontents like my wife, friends, agents, bosses, publishers advise me I have never quite conquered. I am, these insensitive dolts inform me, stubborn. Nothing could be further from the truth. I am only stubborn when I am right and they are wrong.

This teacher advised me of this small flaw in my otherwise superb character. I took heed.

I had discovered, at I guess about age nine, Mark Twain. I understand there are some people who do not believe that Mark Twain was God, but number me not among these heretics. It was balm to my soul to discover him, because I had previously thought that James Fenimore Cooper and Washington Irving were supposed to be writers. The day I found Mark Twain's essay about the literary offenses of Cooper was the day *I* came of age, whatever the vital statistics say.

It was unfortunately about then that this wonderful teacher told the class that by such and such a date we would be expected to have read "The Pathfinder." I rose to my feet and declined to do so. On direct examination, I averred that the reason I would not do so was because I had tried Cooper, found him wanting, and in summation, communicated in the most moderate terms, my belief that he was not a very good writer.

I said he was a lousy writer and I would not read him.

After a brief recess and the clearing of the courtroom, I was induced to add that Mark Twain thought so too.

I was informed by the judge that, my objections notwithstanding, I was banished from school and I could not return until I had opened my mind sufficiently to admit the possibility of giving Cooper a second chance.

I did not feel that he deserved that much of me.

It is always the fact that in all the crises of a child's life, he can remember where it happened, the names of all the participants, the events leading up to the crime, the sentencing—but never the execution. What happened after that, I do not know, but I know that my parents were not summoned to the school, that I did not stay home even one whole day—there would have been no way of explaining that to my mother—that I eventually returned to the school, that I went on loving and crucifying the teacher, and that I never read The Pathfinder. Nor will I do so now.

The moral I draw from this: there's nothing wrong about being stubborn. It's only wrong when you're not right about the thing you're being stubborn about. Like people thinking Cooper could write.

I seem, by some easily explicable psychological quirk, to have passed over Being Sent To The Principal's Office. Our Principal was sixteen feet tall, had tempered steel fingernails, and eyes that I never encountered again until high school, when I first used a Bunsen Burner. His office I never fully recognized until I saw, I think in the German silent movie *Metropolis* or in one of De Mille's early Biblical *opera*, a representation of Moloch. Small naked children were dragged screaming up a flight of stairs and shoveled into a furnace. The only effective difference was that we had to go downstairs, we were prohibited by our code of ethics from screaming, and we went alone. *The Last Mile* was a documentary to us.

At this moment, I can offer no explanation, but it seems evident that we had anticipated Dante and Persephone and Theseus. We went into Hell, were torn apart by the Minotaur, conversed with Pluto, were destroyed and apparently we came back among the living. And without any miserable pomegranate seeds stuck in our teeth, either. And with no help from Virgil or Ariadne. Or anybody.

The Principal shrank to eight feet one day when my best friend, in assembly, pointed out to me that under the table on the platform, the Principal was doing what we didn't know then to call adjusting his clothing. We gave this event some local publicity, and our discovery was confirmed, eventually, by the whole male student body. It was, every assembly day thereafter, an event second in importance only to the Pledge of Allegiance.

Shortly after, a legend was created: some boy, whose name nobody knew, had been grasped in the Principal's talons. In some way, a button had sprung from the boy's coat. A Father, who was twenty-three feet tall, had appeared in the Principal's office, with needle and thread, a gun with Maxim silencer, muscles like Charles Atlas, and a clear record of forty-six successive wins (amateur) over Philadelphia Jack O'Brien. Under his eyes, in the presence of the boy, the Principal had sewed the button back on the coat. Thereafter, the Principal skulked along the corridor, passing easily *under* the drinking fountain. From later evidence, it seems clear that he was a harassed middle-aged man with a baritone voice and a master's degree.

There were other minor punishments, in the first few grades, like Deprivation of Scissors, Standing in the Corner, Refusal on the Part of the Teacher to Read Another Chapter, and Being Sent to Sit With Girls.

"Where did you go?" "OUT."

I bearded my littler boy the other day to find out what punishments prevailed now in the third grade. By the time I explained to him what the word punishment meant, it was time for Disneyland. He doesn't know Mark Twain is God. He thinks Walt Disney is. He's pretty damn stubborn about it, too. I found him later in bed, and for a minute or two sat at his feet and asked for information again. As I understand it, she tells them to keep quiet, and if they do not she asks them again. And again. And again. He was sort of sleepy, but he put up with my idiocy long enough to advise me that once she had scolded them—but not as hard as his mother or his father. I went downstairs and sat on the front steps. It was reassuring to find out that stars still come out at night.

The following day I asked him about Being Sent To Sit With Girls. He likes to sit with girls. I have stopped worrying about this child. For a while. Then, will I give a worry!

There is a man in our town, and he is wondrous wise. All I know about him is that he is reported to have said in conversation that the trouble with kids nowadays is that there are no vacant lots. He must be a good man, and I am sure he must mean by vacant lot the same thing I do. The first thing to understand is that the only thing a vacant lot was vacant of was a house. Outside of that minor lack, a vacant lot was the fullest place you ever saw. Officially, I suppose, we lived in our houses. When challenged by authority for vagrancy, we gave our street address. My recollection is that I lay on my back in my baby carriage, sucking my thumb and waiting to be sprung from the thralldom of Mother and Nurse and goo-goo, so that I could learn to walk and talk and join my peers in stealing lumber to build a hut on the vacant lot.

At the beginning, there were two vacant lots. One across the street, and one at the corner. I was in the stage of running at the nose and being told to go away and not be a pest, of being told to fa crise sake get outa the waya the ball, of being urged to gowanhomeyermotherwantsya, of, on rare occasions, being allowed to chase a ball across the street and run back with it and deliver it to an eight-year-old giant, of being rounded up with the other little kids and herded into a hut and tortured, when they put houses up on that vacant lot. Either I lived on a block full of apprentice sadists or it was the norm, but one of the amusements of the bigger kids, when all else failed, was to collect a batch of small ones and tie them up, put ice in their pants, pepper in their nose, tar in their hair. I will deal with this more fully under the heading of Clothesline.

In any event, by the time I was a full-fledged citizen, the vacant lot was the one at the corner. Its first feature was a rockpile. I am trying very earnestly to figure out whether the rockpile was the remains of an ancient foundation, or the debris of an unfinished foundation. I lean towards the latter, or possibly some contractor had a load of stone left over, or a load of stone to haul away from a blasting, and dumped it on the vacant lot.

We didn't know. It was there. Didn't everybody have a vacant lot on the corner, and wasn't a vacant lot a lot with no house and a rockpile on it?

The rockpile was shaped roughly like the crater of a volcano. We mostly sat on the rim, and we mostly built fires at the bottom. It was, roughly, three miles across from lip to lip when I first went there. Later on, it got smaller. The lot itself had a path through it hacked out of the living jungle, and about halfway through there was a rock too big to take out of the path, and this very minute I can feel my ankle twisting in the sneaker with the black circle over the ankle bone.

I don't suppose bamboo is native to New York State, but how else is there to explain the trees that lined the path, way over my head? Later on, some sort of blight struck this plant. It never again grew so tall. I don't know what sort of plant it was. It was the plant that grew on the vacant lot. It was thicker than a pencil and less thick than a broomstick, and it never was green. It was always off-white and dry, it burned with a lot of smoke, and it was called "scribblage." That is to say, the plant was not called scribblage. The stuff was called that, it was a generic term, something like the word junk. That's it. Junk was manufactured. Scribblage was vegetable junk. Scribblage was used to line the bottom of the rockpile, to hide valuables

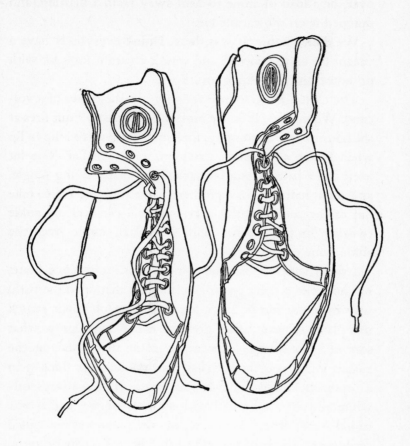

underneath a pile of, to make the tops of deadfalls with, to lay over Tarzan. In short lengths, it was used to smoke, like a cigar.

A horrid suspicion dawns on me. Years and years and years later I was riding down a country road outside of Kansas City, and upon inquiry was told that we were swinging down a lane bordered with marijuana. No—it couldn't be. This was scribblage.

Tarzan of the Apes lived on that lot. I was cavalier a few lines before. We were never so familiar as to call him just plain Tarzan—it was always Tarzanoftheapes. For the benefit of the misguided youth who encounter this . . . the real, the original, the blown-in-the-bottle Tarzanoftheapes was not Elmo Lincoln or Johnny Weismuller or any of their heirs and assigns. Tarzanoftheapes was not a character in a comic strip or in a radio or television show. He was a creature of the imagination, sketched out by Edgar Rice Burroughs with (as we found out later) a more-than-generous unwilling assist from Rudyard Kipling, at fifty cents a throw. In books. Burroughs created a workable sketch: it was fleshed, given spirit and body and habitation by us. In a very real sense, Tarzanoftheapes existed; during the day he was Mitch, the kid next door, who had muscles and a disregard for broken bones. At night he was me, who had less muscles, but more imagination. I ad-libbed Tarzanoftheapes. With Mitch it went strictly according to the book. Once in a while, Mitch would let me be Tarzanoftheapes during the daytime, but there was no percentage in that. I knew Mitch was really Tarzanoftheapes.

Tarzanoftheapes lived on the vacant lot. Huckleberry Finn—Mitch might be Tarzan, but I was Huck—built his raft on the vacant lot. Let's get this straight. I mean a real raft, made out of wood: we had a little trouble locating the Mississippi, but over in Hunt's Woods there was a brook, which almost floated the raft, just as it almost floated the boat I made with the kid who lived on the other side. That was when we were real little. The boat was simple to the point of imbecility. It was an orange crate, with half-inch openings between the boards. The oars were broomsticks with shingles tacked on.

We knew it wasn't a boat, at the same time that we knew that it *had* to be a boat. We needed a boat so bad. We worked on it so hard. We hauled it all the hell and gone to Hunt's Woods, which was roughly halfway across the continent. We put it in the water, we both climbed in, that's how little we were, and the stream was so low it grounded instantly, water poured in from the bottom and sides, the shingles came unstuck from the broomsticks—and yet, I cannot tell you how, because I am, it says here, no longer a child, Simon and I came back perfectly convinced that we had built a boat. And perfectly clear in another section of our minds that we had hauled an orange crate ten blocks and stuck it in a muddy brook and gotten wet up to our armpits and were going to catch hell from our folks and scorn from our contemporaries.

"What did you do?" "NOTHING."

Let's get back to the lot. Tarzanoftheapes, Mowgli, Huck
Finn, the Boy Allies, the Motor Boys, Joe Bonomo, General Pershing, Theodore Roosevelt, Tom Swift, Mitch,
Simon, Mitch's kid brother, Simon's kid brother and I lived
in that lot. We went home for meals, for bed, and for jawing. We went to school because it was The Law. The rest
of the time, we built a hut. What Roosevelt and Mowgli
did with their evenings I haven't the vaguest idea.

When I was a kid, the way you built a hut was this: some
kid would, in his wanderings, come back to the block bust-
ing with news. We would skulk over to the rockpile, exchange fourteen or fifteen passwords, swear eleven or
twenty lifetime vows, and put our heads together. We
whispered. There was nobody within a radius of half a
block, but we whispered because it was a secret. I still think
that's right.

What the kid had found out was that somewhere in town,
a new house was going up. This meant two things to us.

First, it meant that for some time, whenever we didn't
know what to do with ourselves, we could go over and
watch the men building a house. That was entirely wonderful: the equivalent with today's kids, I guess, would be—
well, the mind boggles. Three weeks at Los Alamos, I
guess, with Jackie Gleason.

You could see men with wheelbarrows push a wheel-
barrow across a plank that spanned an excavation. The
plank went up and down very satisfactorily. It looked as if
the men would fall off, perhaps *under* a wheelbarrowful of

cement. They never did, but we hoped. You could watch men mixing cement, in the biggest container any of us had ever seen. What a boat *that* would have made! You could see them make the mound of sand, and scoop a crater out of the top, and pour in the cement from the bag (a smoke screen, like in *The Boy Allies*), and stir in the water and take a hoe and paddle for hours in this beautiful slop, like they kept telling us at home not to do with our gravy and mashed potatoes. You could see men hit a nail every time, and drive a nail home in three strokes.

You could hear Italian being talked, you could see men climbing ladders and getting powdered absolutely white with cement, you could see muscles bulging and heavy things being lifted. You could smell sweat, and hear swearing such as you had never heard before, and guys hollering at each other until they turned purple.

You could sit on the sidewalk and be close enough to touch a man eating a sandwich made out of a whole loaf of bread. You could see a man climb to the ridgepole and tack on a green bough, and then you could see a whole lashing of cementy, garlicky, spitting, nose-blowing between the fingers onto the ground, laughing, hollering brown-moustached men drinking whiskey out of a bottle, water out of a hose, beer out of a barrel, wine out of a jug.

We sat on the sidewalk, and once in a while they swore at us, and one day—surely the greatest day in the history of the world—one of the men gave me a bite of his sandwich.

"What did you do?" "NOTHING."

He also gave me a small green object shaped like a fat leaf. It was an Italian hot pepper, and the inside of my mouth turned to fire and the tears ran out of my eyes. But I got to drink out of the very hose the men had been using, and they didn't laugh for more than three hours.

We sat and watched them, and every day when we went home we went to the rockpile and gave the passwords and swore the oaths, and we split to nobody about the new house. Because every day, sitting there we were thinking about the other thing that a new house going up meant to us.

It meant that we could steal. For our hut. Willie Sutton or Dillinger never planned a heist better. We had to time it close to the end of the construction, because like all criminals, we had to justify our crime. Had we stolen when the house was still going up, it was possible that we might take something that was needed for the house. That was clearly immoral. We were one with Robin Hood and W. C. Fields. We planned to steal from the rich and give to the poor. "What poor, Daddy?" "Us poor." We knew the day, just like we knew the day when immies stopped and baseball started.

It was usually summer, and the evenings were long. It was hot, and there were scratch meals up and down the block, and you could get out on the block early. You could skulk down to where the new house was, you could nonchalantly stroll to the corner, pretending you were not aware you were dragging an express wagon behind you. We were superb actors, aided in no small measure by the total lack of an audience, other than ourselves.

At the corner, we synchronized our heads (lacking watches) and were off. From there on out it was the sack of Rome.

We stole shingles, shingle nails, two by fours, once a keg, a whole keg, of nails, we loaded our pockets, our shirts, our knickerbockers (now, see, there's another thing about kids today; assuming there was anything to steal, without knickers, where the hell would they carry their loot?). We stole siding, we stole rolls of tarpaper, lengths of pipe, pieces of stone, almost empty cement sacks, once we got a box of hinges and a linoleum knife—the most lethal-looking weapon man has ever made. We hooked doorknobs and scraps of cable, push-buttons and tiles, wallpaper and faucet handles.

We took anything that was not nailed down. And that was, literally, the test.

What we took was what was left over. Anything we didn't take, that night, was going back somewhere into limbo. It would not exist any more. We were doing them a favor. We were cleaning up. We were public-spirited citizens. We were heroes.

We went back to the lot by different routes, we stashed our loot. We went home and when somebody said, "Where were you?" we said, "Out," and when somebody said,

"What did you do?" "NOTHING."

"What were you doing until this hour of night?" we said, as always, "Nothing."

Tomorrow we would build our hut.

I'm sorry. It is not yet time to build the hut. First we have to build the treehouse.

The treehouse comes first because we built it first, and I know this because we built the tree house in my backyard, and we must have built it there because we were not yet allowed on the vacant lot.

The other day, on my way to the parkway, I passed a house that had a yard, and in the yard there was a tree, and in the tree there was a treehouse.

And that treehouse was built by a carpenter. It had a floor, made of tongue-and-groove boarding, it had sides built of siding, it had a roof made of a new tent.

It was probably built from a plan by a carpenter. It probably has wrought-iron furniture in it, and a Rouault print on the wall.

There were no kids in it.

We didn't build treehouses that way. We hooked a hammer and we hooked some nails—do you suppose kids still straighten bent nails on a rock?—and we hooked some pieces of wood and a saw.

We cut a piece of wood and reached as high up as we could with one foot, and there we nailed a crosspiece. It took *us* more than three strokes to drive a nail home. We stood on this crosspiece and reached as high up as we could

(71)

with our hands and nailed a crosspiece up there. One kid hung from his hands by that crosspiece while we measured where his feet hung with his knees drawn up. We nailed a crosspiece there. We kept on doing this until we got seventy million feet in the air, where the first crotch of the tree was.

We horsed a couple of pieces of wood in place in the crotch and leaned against the branch, and then we got a piece of awning and bulled that on the crotch somehow; we let down a piece of string with a basket on it, and hauled it up and down with messages, pieces of Tootsie Roll, and eventually, a kitten, just like in all the calendar drawings.

What we wanted was, of course, a rope ladder, so that once up we could haul it in, and be safe from any sort of intrusion. This was beyond our powers.

We were so high up in the empyrean we were on a level with the bedroom windows. You may think this was only one story up in the air. How, then, do you account for the fact that the air was thin, and we were continually surrounded by eagles?

THE trouble with the treehouse was that, little though we were, we could not for long convince ourselves that it was a house. It wasn't, and we knew it after what may have been days or weeks or months —time is a very flexible thing with kids. I know today that I could not possibly have stared at my first cricket for more than minutes, and yet today in that length of time I could write a whole first act. The treehouse after a certain length of time was only a couple of boards and a piece of awning loosely attached to a tree.

But the hut; well, that was a place where we could live. I have been trying hard to remember just how we started to build it. Certainly there was no foundation. I seem to remember building the first wall in one piece, boards and tar-paper hammered onto a couple of two-by-fours, and the two-by-fours extending below, the whole structure raised and the extensions going into holes, and rocks being jammed around. I imagine we got the second wall up the same way, and ran roof beams across the top so that it stood up. The roof, if memory serves, and I am getting pretty dubious about that, was something that was lying around the lot. An abandoned cellar door, perhaps.

I am lying a little now—hell, I am lying a lot. I don't really remember building the hut. I remember repairing it, and expanding it, and putting a better door in it, a hasp and a lock. I remember packing rocks from the rockpile around the perimeter, to strengthen the hut—it was by then a fortress—against any attack. I remember tamping down the dirt floor, and finding a piece of linoleum and a gunny sack to brighten the corner which was mine.

I suppose, when I come right down to it, none of us could stand upright in the hut, and I have a kind of notion that when there were more than two of us in it, no one of us could move.

This is a hell of a note, on an August afternoon in my declining years to realize that really, that hut, that shining palace, that home away from home, that most secure of all habitations, was not much bigger than a big doghouse, and could have been pushed over by an angered Shetland pony. (Which any of us were going to get any moment, or a magic lantern, as soon as we had sold thirty-four million packages of blueing.)

No matter. It was ours. It belonged to us. And if you were not one of us, you could not come in. We had rules, oh Lord, how we had rules. We had passwords. We had oaths. We had conclaves.

It was a pitiful wreck of a tarpaper hut, and in it I learned the difference between boys and girls, I learned that all fathers did that, I learned to swear, to play with myself, to sleep in the afternoon, I learned that some people were Catholics and some people were Protestants and some people were Jews, that people came from different places. I learned that other kids wondered, too, who they would have been if their fathers had not married their mothers, wondered if you could dig a hole right to the center of the earth, wondered if you could kill yourself by holding your breath. (None of us could.)

I learned that with three people assembled, it was only for the briefest interludes that all three liked each other. Mitch and I were leagued against Simon. And then Simon and I against Mitch. And then—but you remember. I didn't know then just how to handle that situation. I still don't. It is my coldly comforting feeling that nobody still does, including nations, and that's what the trouble with the world is. That's what the trouble with the world was then—when Mitch and Simon were the two and I was the one.

What else did I learn in the hut? That if two nails will

not hold a board in place, three will probably not either, but the third nail will split the board. I think kids still do that. I think objects made of wood by children, left to their own devices, if such there be, will assay ten percent wood, ninety percent nails.

I learned that I could lift things, rocks mostly, that my mother would have thought too heavy for me.

I learned to smoke, first, cornsilk wrapped in newspaper. I can taste it to this day. We never had the patience to let the cornsilk really dry. I don't imagine kids do that very much any more, mostly because they've never heard of it. What you do is take the cornsilk, spread it out in the sun until it is brown, like the little beard you find in the husk. Wrap it in a spill of newspaper—it'll look more like a very small ice-cream cone than anything else—set fire to the end, being careful not to torch off your eyebrows. My recollection is that it bore no relationship to tobacco, but it wasn't bad at all. It had one big virtue. When caught, you had not committed a sin, as you did later when you smoked real cigarettes. Real cigarettes stunted your growth, we knew that. What that meant to us was that your growth stopped, right there. It was not impeded. You just plain stopped growing, as if you were frozen. You would be three feet tall when you were sixty years old. It was in no way contradictory that we never saw a grownup three feet tall. They had never smoked as children, and certainly the ones who had were not going to walk around in the daylight letting everybody know what *they* had done.

And to make this intellectual adjustment absolutely complete, we were able to hold this certain knowledge, this fact, intact and at the same time, as soon as possible, start smoking cigarettes.

Before that we smoked scribblage, like cigars. That was pretty bad.

Getting cigarettes was quite a problem. Most of the fathers on our block smoked cigars or pipes, and so far as we knew, no woman smoked. There were no vending machines. Getting cigarettes involved suborning some kid between childhood and adulthood, and the blackmail he thereafter commanded was too expensive. You could then buy cigarettes in little cardboard boxes of ten. You could theoretically, but the man in the store would not sell them to us, no matter how earnestly we told him a father, an uncle, some man on the corner, had asked, nay, commanded us to purchase them. Kids on the wrong side of the tracks could buy them, one at a time, from an open box that storekeepers used to keep on their counters. Three for a penny, was it, or a penny apiece?

It didn't matter. We were on the right side of the tracks. We could not buy, borrow, or beg them. So we stole them.

We did, as a matter of course, considerable stealing.

There were two kinds of stealing: there was the kind of

stealing that we had to do continually for survival; we knew it was stealing, and we had been told it was wrong, but we could see no way of obtaining certain necessities without stealing, so we called it something else. Hooking, pinching, borrowing—which last we occasionally called loaning, just to complicate the situation. I guess that was an even finer distinction, now that I come to think of it; occasionally, of course, we did really borrow things. Therefore, the kind of stealing we would have liked to soften by calling "borrowing" we had to call "loaning."

We pinched food: potatoes to roast on a scribblage-and-wood fire at the hut. They were not exactly roasted: they were put in the fire until black on the outside, when they were called mickies. They were then broken open and seasoned with stolen salt. At home, we were accustomed to put butter on potatoes, but for some reason it never occurred to us to hook butter for the mickies. They were totally carbonized on the outside, quite raw on the inside. I remember them as being nasty and wonderful at one and the same time, and perhaps the best part of it was that often there were little worms of red fire still running around the skin, while we ate the barely cooked, terribly hot inside. We hooked apples to cook the same way, but they were not very good. We hooked sugar lumps, which we had been told would give us worms. Candy was not so much stolen as taken as a birthright.

We stole medicine: it was the days of great, epic, and

constant purging, and there were many medicines which came in powders. They lay in a little cardboard box, little carefully folded stiff tissue-paper enclosures, like odd and unique handmade envelopes, half of the packets red, half blue. I suppose they were Seidlitz powders, I heard them talked about then, I think they were cathartic, but I have not heard of them since I was a kid, and I do not really know. What we did know was that if you put first one colored envelope, then the other, into a bottle of water, there was considerable action. We dared each other to drink them, but I don't recall that any of us took the dare. My kids display the same sort of interest in Alka-Seltzer, and they put a thumb over an opened bottle of Coke and shake, as we did with pop. Pop came much later in my years: Mother had a great belief in natural things; honey was better than sugar, fresh fruit was better than candy, figs and nuts were better than cookies. Outside of milk, the only thing us kids got that came in bottles—with the single horrible exception of citrate of magnesia—was grape juice. Citrate of magnesia was the children's purge: I would gladly have been strung up by my thumbs for two days rather than endure the horrible, jawclenching torture of magnesia, and when my grandfather brightly announced that to him it was just like lemon soda, I could have strung *him* up by the thumbs. However, there was no escape, and sooner or later, you emptied the bottle, which I recall as containing a bathtubful.

One other thing in the more or less medicinal line we always planned to steal was a seltzer siphon: it was a stomach-centered world in those days, and physicking was that time's constant preoccupation as ours is tranquilizing drugs. The seltzer bottle stood on many tables, and was sovereign incitement to what was then not called burping, because indeed it was belching. Our purpose in stealing it was to spray one another with it. Now, in this halcyon age, my children can tune in television and watch one expensive wit doing it to another. Us kids never, as I recall it, ever got away with the theft of a seltzer bottle. We had to content ourselves as well as we could with spitting on one another.

But back to larceny: we loaned chalk from the school, money from our mothers, golf balls from smaller children, clothesline from anywhere. Truly, I will get to clothesline pretty soon.

That was the loaning, the hooking, the pinching. The money we took from our mothers was not stealing, because it was money that was laying around. On kitchen tables, bureaus, mantelpieces. That was, like at the new house, not nailed down and it was not stealing.

The other kind of stealing was honest-to-God stealing, and we did that in a different way, knowing that we were committing criminal acts, scared, awaiting the arrival of the police, and pretty damn proud of ourselves. Money that was not laying around came in that category. If a pocket-book was laying around, but it was closed, taking money out of it was stealing, and we did that only on extreme provocation. Extreme provocation was when (And do you remember your schoolteacher forbidding you to ever start a sentence that way—or split an infinitive to boot—or use dashes as punctuation?) we had been denied our birthright, to wit, a lethal weapon. This was, most often, a bee-bee gun, next most often a hunting knife, next most often, fireworks. I never got a gun or a knife. In Mexico, at age twenty-eight, I bought the goddamnedest folding machete you ever saw, last month in an Army-Navy store I got me an air pistol that shoots bee-bees, slugs *and* darts, and if anybody knows where you can buy those little Chinese firecrackers in red paper, the ones about the size of a little finger, the wicks all braided together, ready for unbraiding to make them last longer, for bending to make into sizzlers, communications to my publisher will be greatly appreciated. I know where *you* can still buy realies.

The obtuseness of parents is incredible (and I can hear my own kids saying, "But of course"), but I never got a bee-bee gun or a hunting knife when I was a kid, because my parents said they were too dangerous. And well they are. But how, then, was it allowable that we had a dart board and darts, and I tell you I ground those points on the front steps to better than a needle point, and any time we wanted we could go borrow—and I mean really borrow—the ice pick? The ice pick was usually so sharp it could not be honed any better. It was the universal handy-dandy all-combination tool, for making holes in anything, and after you had used it for boring a hole in a belt to strap a kid to a tree to play Indians burning settlers, it was good for an hour of throwing into the garage wall, *thunk*. About darts: we used to get a kitchen match, loan ourselves a needle, force the needle into one end of the match and bind it with loaned black thread. The other end was split, and two little wings of paper folded in. This was a dart that stuck to anything, including other children's clothes, and occasionally other children. I shudder to think of it.

So we stole for our arsenal, like the Irish rebels, and we got nowhere.

We stole for lust, too: this dodge I remember with pride. The days I look at the typewriter and curse my misguided career, I think of the cigar-store caper and dream I had followed it up. Today I could have been a successful gangster, with personal barbers and beautiful disposable broads appearing and disappearing one after the other like tissues in a Kleenex box, a permanent table at some fancy night club, an assistant hood to drive and park my car, pack my bags—oh, well.

I don't know what age I was when I discovered naked ladies, but I remember where. At the barber shop, and in the Police Gazette. When I go to the barber shop today, I have to burrow down through Bugs Bunny and Little Lulu, Mumsy Moose and Addle the Aardvark and Truly

"What did you do?" "NOTHING."

Bestial Horror Comics to find the newspaper, but in those days, a little boy walked into the barber shop and sat down and kept his mouth shut, and there was no equity about your turn: if there were men around, you waited until they were through. And you didn't run around saying, "Yang yang," the way kids do in a barber shop now, and having fond fathers smile at you. Open your kisser, and you were melted down to a small puddle by the assembled glares.

So I kept my mouth shut and looked at the naked ladies in the Police Gazette. Then I sat in the barber chair and looked at the naked lady—she was usually an Indian lady, and not completely naked—on the calendar.

That's where I found out about naked ladies, and so did the other kids, and after a while it occurred to us that if the barber, Lou Kahler the Square-Deal man (and that was no political slogan) could get these magazines, we could too.

There was a candy, cigar, stationery, toy, newspaper, rubber band, rubber ball, chewing gum, poker and pinochle card, library-paste store which we honored with our patronage. In the back was a large rack of magazines. We entered the store, and one of our outposts dickered with Mr. Cantor over some licorice whips, and chocolate sponge. The rest of us proceeded to the magazine rack. One of us got down the *Saturday Evening Post*, a magazine in which we had absolutely no interest, except that it cost a nickel and was large. In that magazine, every few pages, we introduced other reading matter. *Film Fun, College Life* (not

(83)

"Where did you go?" "OUT."

College Humor—that had jokes, this had girls) *Captain Billy's Whiz Bang, Physical Culture* (don't be silly, it had naked *ladies,* too), and whatever other instructive and edifying reading matter we could find. I took this lustful sandwich under my arm, and even more debonair than Jimmy Valentine, I strolled in a cosmopolitan way down the aisle of the store, past the petty playthings of children, gave Mr. Cantor a nickel, and then, boy did we run for that hut. I don't suppose I have the nervous system now to do this once, and some tiresome hanger-on of my youth will claim that I didn't do it even then, but you know how people will knock down a successful criminal. I know I did it half a dozen times, and the last time was not even worried about Mr. Cantor. It was foolproof. Of course, a year or so ago I passed his store and I don't believe I went in. Just didn't feel like it, that's all.

However.

In the hut we looked and we learned. And drooled. I remember a picture of Clara Bow with one shoulder strap—and then there was Toby Wing—and look at Lily Damita—she's bending *way* over.

Allow me to assure you that I will never lust after anything in my life as I did in the hut after the girl who played in the Wheeler and Woolsey pictures. I tell you, she didn't wear practically anything. Did she, Mitch?

I don't believe my kids will have to hook those magazines: first, because I don't believe any of them exists any more; and second because the last time I looked at the *Saturday Evening Post,* a lady was deploring brilliantly and quite rightly, I thought, the depravity of the Cannes Film Festival, and in case anyone wondered what depravity she was talking about, there was a profusion of photographic bosom that would have made *Film Fun* look like *St. Nicholas.*

Now the old man is really snarling: when I was a kid, there was a difference between respectable and disrespectable, even a distinction between good and bad, and that seems to have gone by the board along with Concord grapes and sickle pears (don't give me that Seckel pear jazz) and Country Gentleman corn and blackberries with grit and taste in them, pullet eggs and stiff farmer cheese. There were two kinds of magazines: one with pictures of naked ladies in it, therefore bad, therefore enjoyable. There was another kind of magazine with stories about dogs that everybody thought were chicken-killers but were not, about young men who invented new kinds of carburetors and married the boss's daughter with freckles on her nose, with editorials that were in praise of America, all America, every bit of it, both sides and top and bottom, to and fro and hither and yon and upwards and onwards; where the illustrations were drawn so that you could count every hair in Grandma's head as she threw her hands up and said, "Laws!"; where the good guys were clean-shaven and the pure girls were blonde: therefore these magazines were good; therefore intermittently tolerable, only occasionally enjoyable.

Before that, there had been *John Martin's Big Book*, which was so wonderful I cannot begin to tell you about it, and *St. Nicholas*, which my sisters liked.

But at this age, when we lived in the hut and smoked cigarettes and honed after Renée Adorée (pronounced, of course, Reenee A-door-ee) we were Sinn Feiners and Revisionists and Bolsheviks in our souls, we wanted big muscles and big guns and big knives, we were, and I am not making fun, enemies of society and we needed things that were bad more than we needed cod-liver oil. And let me tell you, we had opponents worthy of our steel; the day came when I was walking to school and somebody said I would not smoke out there on the street, so of course I did, and you know that the lady who lived at the top of the hill on Primrose Avenue called my old lady, and I caught several kinds of hell. The lady on Primrose had not even the slightest quaver of doubt at calling my mother; I was a child, I had, every day on my way to school, played the game with the other kids of standing up in front of her hedge with my back to it, putting my arms out wide, and falling back like a felled tree. She had hollered at us for doing it, we had run to avoid identification, she knew I was her and her hedge's enemy, and first chance she got to get even, she did.

But here's the point: that left me free to ruin her hedge

and smoke cigarettes, both delightful occupations. My kids can't break any grown-up statutes, and hear the delightful noise of shackles breaking, because they can't find out what laws there are to break. Let me settle the problem of juvenile delinquency once and for all, because I happen to know: the reason these kids are getting in trouble with cops is because cops are the first people they meet who say, and mean it, "You can't do that."

If there's anything in the world kids need, it's rules. When I was a kid, we honest-to-God did the business of drawing a line on the ground and if a kid wanted to fight, he had a choice, to step over the line or not. There it was. No more argle-bargle, step over the line, and pow. Or, stay on your side of the line. Keep the knife in your pocket in school and keep it. Take it out and lose it. Come in the house this minute, or straight to bed when I catch you.

When my kids were smaller, their mother and I had been washed in the blood of, God save the mark, permissive upbringing. We privately, or at least I privately, thought it was a crock, particularly when I observed that my first-born had permission to take his bottles at any time, provided those times were two, four, six, two—or whatever the hell hours they were. And his nap was entirely at his discretion as long as it was when his parents were totally exhausted.

He soon learned that he could do anything he wanted as long as what he wanted was what we wanted. Which is a fact of life, between parents and kids. But when their little heads first deal with problems of more complicated decisions, when parents begin to wonder if they have the right to make decisions for them, when those same parents know they have an obligation to, it gets a little harder. But not as hard as all that.

I can no longer remember the crisis which involved my son: but in essence, it had reached the point, the point of all arguments, when he was saying the hell he would and I was saying the hell he wouldn't. I don't know—go to bed, or get out of bed, or come in from the garden or get the hell out into the garden.

He was two or three. His mother rushed in to say that I must Gesell him a little, or at least Spock him or treat him with a little Ilg, and I went away. To bed, or out of bed, into the garden or out of the garden. She then left him to his own devices.

I found him later, ready to renew hostilities, but on his face and in his manner was much weariness, much fatigue, and a kind of desperation. I had a moment of pure illumination: I stood there and saw inside his head as clearly as if there had been a pane of glass let in his forehead. What he was saying was, "Please, please, for Heaven's sake, somebody come and take this decision out of my hands, it's too big for me."

I grabbed him and picked him up and carried him to

wherever it was I thought he was supposed to go. He was little then, he hit me and bit me and wet me, he hollered bloody murder and did his level best to kill me. I remember now, it was to his bed he was supposed to go. I got him there, and dumped him in, put the crib side up. He was in his cage, and he had been put there by his keeper, and he went to sleep as happy as ever I saw him. There were rules. Nobody was going to leave him out in the middle of nowhere trying to figure out what he was supposed to do, when he was too young to know what to do.

The lady at the top of Primrose tipped off the domestic cops, and there was a rule established. The rule was, don't smoke on your way to school when you are eleven years old and people on Primrose Avenue know who you are.

So we stole *Film Fun*, and read it in the hut, and absorbed from each other the most intoxicating misinformation about ladies, naked and otherwise.

Among the other things that were clearly and demonstrably good and bad were books. Good books were books that came from the library. Bad books were books that came from other kids. We always liked bad books, and only sometimes liked good books.

This had nothing at all to do with naked ladies, and oddly enough, it had nothing to do with the contents of the books. Henty came from the library. Certainly, *The Cat of Bubastes* was as good a book as anybody had ever written.

"Where did you go?" "OUT."

The title alone was one of the best things ever written. Washington Irving was a stinker, from the library or from home.

Good books were either library books or birthday presents. Bad books were fifty cents apiece, new, and were tradeable. Bad books were *The Boy Allies, The Motor Boys, Tom Swift,* Sax Rohmer. They were not read so much as devoured. There was an established rate of exchange, and it took at least three *Rover Boys*—they were, for some reason, held in much scorn in my literary circle—for even not the latest *Tom Swift.* The newest *Tom Swift* was read by three people at once, one holding the book and two saying, "Not so fast," or "Come on, fa Crise sake, turn the page."

This lasted only until we found Jules Verne. What a surprise that was, finding out that there was somebody better than Victor Appleton—and in the library, honest, I swear, I'll show ya!

Then an uncle of mine gave me a complete set of Mark Twain, and I was, and am, equipped for life. I started in at Volume One, and read through to the end of Volume Twenty. I concluded that there was very little else of value written down, and I went back to Volume One and started all over again. I have never stopped doing this. I was told the other evening that someone, either Thurber or Mencken, or both, looked forward to old age as sitting on a screened porch reading *Huckleberry Finn.* With, for me, maybe Louis Armstrong playing "Beale Street Blues" in a handy grape arbor, and a jug of Paddy's Irish whiskey like it used to be, close at hand.

However.

I found Mark Twain, and my education as an adult began.

As a kid, I read Dan Beard, *Tanglewood Tales, The Tennessee Shad Stories, Stalky and Company*, and all the rest of Kipling—it is odd, but I cannot remember reading any children's books at all. Not Grimm, or Andersen, or the Blue, Green, Yellow or Puce Fairy Stories. The only book I can remember having read to me was some crud called *Bobby and the Big Road*, which I strongly suspect was the natural ancestor of all those woolly-bear books the kids get now. It was read to me on the supposition, I have no doubt, that since I was called Bobby, I would identify with the presumed hero of the book. This was an oaf, who, by all that's holy, tripped over shadows. A fat chance of letting myself get mixed up with a schlemiel like that.

We did have a set of books for children: it was called "The Boys' and Girls' Bookshelf" and that I read from Volume One to Volume Whatever it was, and I remember only one thing from it.

There was a photograph of some square in some foreign city: there was a fenced-off grass park, and on the road at the right, otherwise deserted, was a hansom cab coming down the street. I used to stare and stare at this picture, why I cannot tell you, and one day I saw the horse and

"Where did you go?" "OUT."

carriage move. I reported this information to a sister—I was very small—and she informed me that this was not possible. I then concluded that it was unwise to tell important things to sisters.

There was another book, of which all I remember is that there was a frontispiece illustration, in color, called "The Garden of the Birds." Do not ask me what that had to do with the book. Then, it *was* the book. They were very odd-looking birds, some with tails that would have pulled them ass-over-tea-kettle, some with heads they would have had to trip over (like a bull-terrier pup next door, that, so help me, used to gallop along until its head overbalanced it and then somersaulted), and all the birds stood on little stick legs that, I seem to recall, had no feet, but were just stuck into green grass. This was before I could read, and for reasons that are quite inexplicable to me now, there was enough in this picture to keep me studying it for months.

To find out how the birds were supposed to work, I guess. Or just plain nothing to do.

Because that was the main thing about kids then: we spent an awful lot of time doing nothing. There was an occupation called "just running around." It was no game. It had no rules. It didn't start and it didn't stop. Maybe we were all idiots, but a good deal of the time we just plain ran around.

Many many hours of my childhood were spent in learning how to whistle. In learning how to snap my fingers. In

(92)

hanging from the branch of a tree. In looking at an ants' nest. In digging holes. Making piles. Tearing things down. Throwing rocks at things.

Spitting. Breaking sticks in half. Unplugging storm drains, and dropping things down storm drains, and getting dropped things out of storm drains. (Which we called sewers.) So help us, we went and picked wild flowers. This was Hunt's Woods again. In the spring I went there for violets, and yellow violets, and dogtooth violets, and Jack in the Pulpit, and sometimes Dutchman's breeches, and Indian pipe, the whitest thing I have ever seen in my life, strange and really ghostlike against the black boggy earth. Later, something we called star grass, tiny, intensely blue flowers and the stem triangular, a real wonder. I was a real goof about these things, and on Sundays, when we went for a ride, my sisters used to groan when we passed a clump of tiger lilies, because I made myself a real pest, a thorough kid brother, until the car was stopped and I could gather a bunch. I was looney about flowers.

All of us, for a long time, spent a long time picking wild flowers. Catching tadpoles. Looking for arrowheads. Getting our feet wet. Playing with mud. And sand. And water. You understand, not doing anything. What there was to do with sand was let it run through your fingers. What there was to do with mud was pat it, and thrust in it, lift it up and throw it down.

When it rained, water ran along the curb and we sailed

twigs down the current, built little dams. In the winter, after the snowballs and the snow forts, after the sleds and the toboggans, there was the crusty snow, and there was the (what to call it? Not a game, not a sport, not even a contest)—there was just the *thing* of seeing if you could walk on the crust without breaking through. There was ice-skating, and a kind of primitive hockey, and we made slides on the sidewalk and damn near broke our necks, and then some grownup came out and spread ashes on it, and we grumbled. But there was also just the thing of standing on a frozen place on land and breaking the ice delicately by teetering, or even better than that, just rocking there and watching the air bubble slide back and forth under the ice.

There was The Reservoir (which is now a swimming pool, I am told.) It was where we skated, and we never knew how exactly to say it, so we slurred the last syllable. We knew it wasn't "voyer," and "vwah" was way up-town, so we split the difference. But one thing we knew. It was capital T on The and capital R on Reservoir. It was the only one in the world, you see. We played hockey there, we had learned discussions about the various kinds of skates. Double runner, for little kids. Then single runner, that clamped on. Then, for the girls only, figure skates. I had hockey skates, after a while, when I graduated to shoe skates, and ankle supporters, which were shameful and put on so nobody could see. And did no good. What we all wanted was racing tubes, because only the big kids and

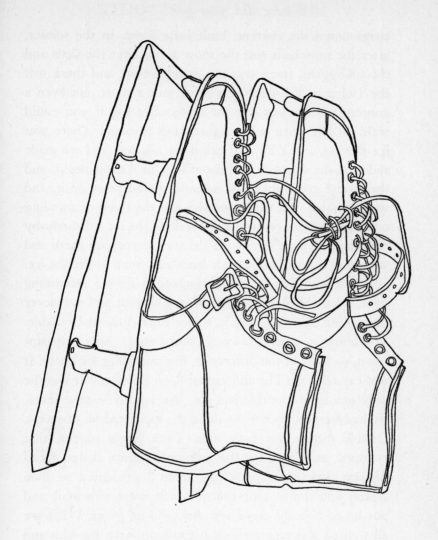

the men had them, and they went around in a fast and
vicious circle in the best part of The Reservoir, crouching,
wearing knitted Balaclavas, crossing their feet on the turns
and making a wonderful noise. We tried to cross our feet
in the rink turn and went upon our behinds many times.
But the best thing I remember about The Reservoir had
nothing to do with skating: it was one day when there was
something called rubber ice, that bent in long waves as you
walked on it. That was something. I never saw it but once.

But about this doing nothing: we swung on swings. We
went for walks. We lay on our backs in backyards and
chewed grass. I can't number the afternoons my best friend
and I took a book apiece, walked to opposite ends of his
front porch, sank down on a glider at his end, a wicker
couch at mine, and read. We paid absolutely no attention
to each other, we never spoke while we were reading, and
when we were done, he walked me home to my house, and
when we got there I walked him back to his house, and then
he—aria da capo.

We watched things: we watched people build houses, we
watched men fix cars, we watched each other patch bicycle
tires with rubber bands. We watched men dig ditches, climb
telephone poles—I can hear the sound now of climbing
irons on a pole, this was a race of heroes!—we watched
trains at the station, shoe-shine men at the station, Italian
men playing *boccie*, our fathers playing cards, our mothers
making jam, our sisters skipping rope, curling their hair.

"Where did you go?" "OUT."

For at least a month I watched my sisters making beads: they cut paper into long triangular strips, put glue on them, wrapped them around hatpins, and then I think they varnished them. I don't recall that they ever wore them, but I'm here to tell you they made them. They also did something called tie-dying: it was a rage, and it produced handkerchiefs of unbelievable ugliness.

We strung beads on strings: we strung spools on strings; we tied each other up with string, and belts and clothesline.

We sat in boxes; we sat under porches; we sat on roofs; we sat on limbs of trees.

We stood on boards over excavations; we stood on tops of piles of leaves; we stood under rain dripping from the eaves; we stood up to our ears in snow.

We looked at things like knives and immies and pig nuts and grasshoppers and clouds and dogs and people.

We skipped and hopped and jumped. Not going anywhere—just skipping and hopping and jumping and galloping.

We sang and whistled and hummed and screamed.

What I mean, Jack, we did a lot of nothing. And let's face it, we still do it, all of us grownups and kids. But now, for some reason, we're ashamed of it. I'll leave the grownups out, but take a kid these days, standing or sitting or lying down all by himself, not actively engaged in any recognizable—by grownups—socially acceptable activity. We want to know what's the matter. That's because *we*

(98)

don't know how to do nothing any more. Kids have got enough sense to roll with the punch, to give in and be a slack-jawed idiot when boredom is afoot, but we can't let them alone. It's the old business of the reformed drunk: we can't do that any more, so we won't let them.

My argument is, of course, that of the physician in England whose cure for the world's ills was simple: everybody go to bed for three days.

Every time I get into an argument these days, somebody jaws me about now look here, you say there is no progress, well how about disease, what do you think it was like in the eighteenth century? What I think it was like—and I am not against progress, I just think we've taken in a lot of crud along with the good, and I'm not sure if they're separable—is that it never occurred to people then that they shouldn't hurt, and therefore it didn't hurt them as much as we, who now know things needn't hurt, think.

We were bored, when we were kids, but we never thought that a day was anything but a whole lot of nothing interrupted occasionally by something. My kids are bored. I was bored. But I didn't know the word.

I know the word all right these days. And the situation. And so do millions of other people, who try to get away from it by furious activity of all sorts. That they never escape it seems only to drive them on to more extended attempts, and they hunt it out of their children with the same intensity, and very much the same results. From long ago when Bea Lillie (or was it Fannie Brice, same words, different accent) did the thing of clobbering a hand-held kid and hollering, "I brought you to the beach to enjoy yourself and by God you're going to enjoy yourself," to the kid I saw at a swimming pool the other day, frog-flippers on his feet, goggles and a snorkel tube on his head, a plastic inflated raft with a clear panel to observe through under one arm, standing at the edge of the shallow end of the swimming pool, there doesn't seem to have been much change. This kid couldn't swim. He was watching, perhaps with envy, certainly with interest, an infant of two or three who stood in a puddle, stamping with her left foot, getting dirty water in freckles all over her.

After a while the infant sat down in the puddle and did nothing. My little boy had gone swimming. My wife had gone swimming. I had gone swimming. We all sat in our own little puddles and did nothing. We were doing nothing. We were not particularly worried about it. That's one of the reasons you come to a swimming pool. To sit on your duffs and swim and after a while, just sit on your duffs. There is a difference between doing nothing and being bored. Being bored is a judgment you make on yourself. Doing nothing is a state of being.

Kids know about this, if you'll leave them be.

It is now time to talk about clothesline.

Clothesline was to my childhood what Scotch tape is to my kids. Clothesline was the universal matter. Clothesline was what, when you decided on any project, you had to find first, unless you were indoors, when what you had to find was a hairpin. This you found by finding your mother.

Clothesline was, for girls, skipping rope. It was used by boys for tying each other, and any girls handy, up. Sometimes this was done against the tyee's will, but almost as often it was done with permission. One of us had seen Houdini, all of us had read about him. We tied each other up to see how long it would take to get free. We tied up prisoners. From time to time, and now I cannot get inside that year's head, we tied each other up just for tying each other up. No game, no revenge, no torture, no acting out. Just tying up, as sometimes we ran around and screamed just for that itself.

Clothesline was used for fastening things together, for example, fastening two kids together, back to back, as above. It was used to harness a batch of little kids together for use as horses with a delivery wagon. It was used the same way with a sled, and sometimes instead of little kids we used the patient collie who lived next door.

Clothesline was used, between the clothespoles in our backyard, as a tightrope. Call me a liar, but there was a time when we thought we could learn to walk a tightrope and we tried it, although despite our best efforts, what we did not learn to walk was a very slack clothesline. It was used as a high-jump standard, and the day one of us found a bamboo pole in the center of a rolled-up rug, it was used as a pole-vault standard too. It was used as a climbing rope, for the ascent of garages, it was used as a belt, as a lasso (which we pronounced then "lassoo" and I learned later is really a lariat, which I still pronounce "larri*et*"), as a part of something we called bolas, a kind of Gaucho "lassoo."

This was made by tying a couple of rocks to both ends of a piece of clothesline. This assembly was whirled around the head and let go, and it wrapped itself around the clothes-pole, other kids, and one's own ankles with equal force and pain.

Clothesline was a sort of natural resource, found in abundance growing in backyards, and it was The Law that when it did not have clothes on it, it was borrowable. It was not permitted to cut it, however, and once it was necessary to cut it, unless it was a very long clothesline and the loss would not show, you had to steal it. Then it was all right for belts and bolas. I just remembered a game of my early childhood, which was to run through the wash, and feel the damp and clean-smelling sheets against one's face. Do *that* with an electric drier! Along with clotheslines, sort of the fruit of this freely growing vine, were clothespins, for which we had a number of uses. In my town, they were the clothespins without springs: they could be made into dolls, they were good for digging, they made fine tent stakes, they could be turned into a sort of primitive pliers, and with the aid of a few strips of wood and a couple of nails, a toy in which two figures with little wooden ham-

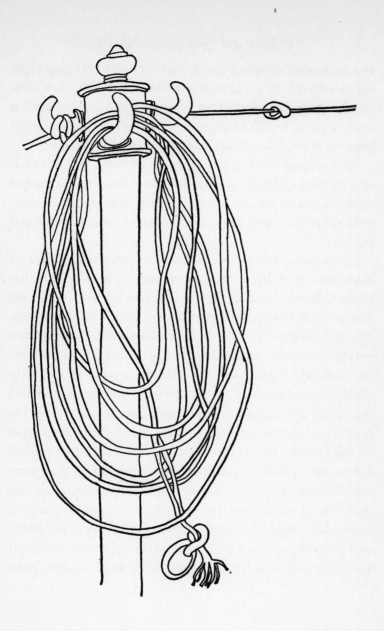

mers struck alternate blows. We thought of clothespins generally as just something good to have a few of stashed away. They were very good-shaped things. Once in a great while we would encounter a spring clothespin: these were real treasures, and were carried clamped on the finger until incipient gangrene set in.

Clothesline was also good for wrapping around things, for practicing knot-tying with, and the frayed end was a very pleasant thing to stroke one's face with. It was pretty fair chewing. I hate to leave this subject, but I have to tell about torture. Torture can wait. I haven't mentioned clothespoles. These were not those upside-down umbrellas you don't see very much any more. These were honest upright poles, set at the corners of a square. They were as big around as my head when I first learned to walk, they had an acorn-shaped turning on top, and a cross pole. They were painted white, and were for a long time a corner in "Puss in the Corner," later home base in hide-and-go-seek. Later on, a big tree was home base, and this tree was, I now realize, one of the many things in my childhood that I knew with a sense that I no longer know anything with. I knew that tree not by sight, or smell; not by location, or height, or kind: I knew that tree by forehead. As I knew the picket fence by sound; the ornamental iron fence outside the Bailey Estate by getting my knee caught in it; the stair banister at home by behind, the red leather chair by coolness on my thighs, the washcloth by taste. Somewhere in here belongs the way your fingers got wrinkled in the bath, when you had stayed too long. And that thing we did, at what age I cannot tell, of running a needle along underneath the skin of our hands. It did not hurt, but it was frightening, and that was part of why we did it.

I seem to have gotten past clothesline and into torture. Very well, there was that kind of self-torture, like with the needle. There was the holding of breath, and the not-blinking of eyes, the drinking of nauseous mixtures, the eating of untried substances, the first corncob pipes, the cigars, the pulls at the wine bottle. It was prohibition, or else we could have done a lot of that.

But I meant the torture of other kids. There was a definite series of tortures, physical ones. I don't mean that general casual torture that all kids practice, like plain hitting, like mud-throwing, isolation. These were things we did to each other to see how well the other kid could stand up. There was the Indian Wrist Burn. This consisted of grabbing another kid's wrist in one's two hands, placed close together. One hand twisted clockwise, the other counter. It hurt like hell.

There was the Indian Scalp Burn. This was done by placing the palm flat against the newly haircutted back of another kid's neck and pushing up against the grain.

There was the Indian Chest Beat. This was usually the climax of wrestling. You had another kid down. In the books like *Tom Brown's Schooldays* you were then supposed to have licked him and would let him up, but in our friendly circle, the minute you let him up he would walk away three or four paces and then jump you or heave a rock at you. It was almost always so with fights when I was a kid. In all the books, the until then mild boy hammered the villain with straight lefts and right crosses until he sank on the ground never to rise again. Our fights didn't work out that way. In the first place, we took turns being the bully, and in the second place, fights never ended. I had a fight with a guy who is now, they tell me, a distinguished physician in my home town. Then he was not. He was a boy named Piggy. I had a fight with Piggy that went on for two months, after school, every day. We were both heartily sick of it, but the other kids thought it was great and Piggy and I hammered each other day after tiresome day.

But the Indian Chest Beat: you were on top. You placed a knee in each of the underdog's elbows, as you sat on his stomach. You beat, alternately with each clenched fist, on his breast bone until he cried or you were tired, or somebody came along. This also hurt like hell.

There was old-fashioned arm-twisting, frog-marching, there was The Drill, the Hammerlock, the Toe Lock, there was a charming thing called Punching the Muscle. This was simple. This involved a series of punches, as hard as possible, in the muscle of the upper arm until a kind of paralysis set in.

"Where did you go?" "OUT."

This last was not always a torture. It was sometimes part
of a game called Two-For-Biting. I understand the heathens
call this two-for-flinching. It went on all the time. It involved walking up to another kid and thrusting your fist in
his face without any warning. If he pulled back, or blinked,
you then said, "Twoferbiting," and hit him in the upper
arm, twice, as hard as you could. He then theoretically
waited until you were off guard, and did the same to you.
If by any chance, he tried and you did not startle, you got
to hit him. If he tried and, banking on your pulling back,
touched you on the face, you got two free shots on him. It
is my feeling that I walked around most of the years of my
childhood with a constant supply of three wounds. A black-
and-blue upper arm from this, a scab on my knee from falling down, a swollen wrist. The wrist was swollen either
from the Indian Wrist Burn or from the choosing game of
scissors-paper-rock.

Now, in this, kids also seem to be different today. I don't
see it going on, and I don't hear about it, and maybe it's just
that I'm being as unseeing as any parent—but I don't think
so. I don't think kids beat up on each other as much as they
used to, just the way you don't see fights between men as
much as you used to. I know all about the crime rate, and
about mugging, but it's my belief that that's different: that's
for money, and it's for keeps, and it's with knives and black-
jacks and guns, but generally I don't think kids get whipped
any more, I don't think as many husbands put the slug on

their wives as used to, and I don't think kids clobber each other as much as they did. I think that's wonderful, unless it means that people deprived of small violence need big violence. Perhaps it means, let us hope, that people unused to violence will never accept it casually. I wouldn't know.

I do know I never liked very much being slugged, and I never liked very much slugging people, and when I was thirteen and tired to death of fighting Piggy, I decided that maybe one of the best things about growing up was you didn't have to fight any more. With fists. I swore a great oath about it. It's been no trouble to keep.

If I were asked—and since it's extremely unlikely that anyone will ever ask me, I propose to ask myself right now —what two objects seem to me now to have bulked the largest in my childhood, my answer would be prompt. Garnets and chestnuts.

I have saved them for the last because that's another thing I did in my childhood, and I wish I could do now—save the best for the last.

I never saw anything more beautiful than my sister's Roman-striped hair-ribbon. I am reconciled at last to never seeing one like it again. Nothing will ever look or taste as good as the Country Gentleman corn I ate, there will never be quite as satisfying a dish as a mound of mashed potatoes and the round spoon making a crater on top and filling it with gravy; I will never feel quite the quality of despair I once felt at flunking algebra, nor will I ever feel quite the same thrill of niceness, eternity, and yes, beauty, as my first—and last—comprehension of Euclid; no book will ever start, " 'Tom!' No answer. 'Tom!' No answer;" I will never smell anything so satisfying as the very first encounter with my own smell as a male, not a boy; no Super-Constellation will ever fly as wonderfully as the first model airplane built from plans in *The American Boy;* I will never have a friend like the friends I had then; I am pretty sure now I will never find an arrowhead.

But all the same, the best for the last: garnets and chestnuts. The rockpile on the vacant lot was composed, perhaps all, surely largely, of what we called and what may have been sandstone, and we found out fairly early that if you pried at it with a knife, you could split it into sheets. There was slate there also, and that could be split in sheets, but by banging, not by splitting. The slate could be chipped into arrowheads, and we made a kind of cave-man knife of it, too. But one day, splitting the sandstone, we found little red nuggets in it. We spent some time, prizing the little nuggets out. Did one of us know then that these were garnets, or did we not know until we showed them to a grownup? It doesn't matter. We knew they were stones, we knew that they were precious stones. When we found the word garnets, we knew that they were precious stones used in jewelry, that they were practically the same as diamonds, that our fortunes were made.

People, grownups, don't know, or don't want to know,

how important money is to little kids. When I see my kids with dough in their kick, I remember quite clearly what cash is to a child. It's like a gun to a man on the frontier; it's an equalizer. My kid sending away to Johnson Smith and Company for a sixty-volt generator and a plate palpitator and a deck of marked cards is bellying up to the bar and naming his own poison. When he hands me the jam jar with the spring snake inside, and I open it and lose two beats of my pulse, he's holding a gun on me, and he's two feet taller than I am.

When we got together enough garnets, we were going to buy a motor buckboard, get a really good Galena crystal and million-ohm earphones, get racing tubes and every Motor Boy book published, buy all our clothes at the Army-Navy store, go to visit Dan Beard and Raymond Ditmars and Breitbart the Strong Man and (just me) Luther Burbank; I was going to stop taking Maltine, nobody was going to chivvy me off the window seat where I was in the balloon with *Tom Sawyer Detective*, and chase me out to get some fresh air; if I wanted a pocket oilstone for my knife, I was going to get it, having passed the age where I thought a flat stone and some spit was really effective; I would have a subscription to *The American Boy, and* to *Boy's Life, and* to *The Open Road, and* to *Popular Science, and* to *Popular Mechanics—and* to *Film Fun, and* to *Captain Billy's Whiz Bang.*

Our parents would be terribly deferent to us, and people

would point us out on the streets as the boys who owned
the garnet mine. Our pictures would be in the paper. We
would be very kind to everybody, and nobody would tell
us what to do. Ever. If our parents told us what to do, we
wouldn't give them any more garnets, we would take away
our brothers' and sisters' Shetland ponies, and put away our
fathers' cigars and brandy, our mothers' jewelry and silk
dresses until they behaved themselves properly.

We chipped away like prisoners on a rockpile, and we
stashed our garnets away in matchboxes: we would have
made a cache out of them, but we didn't know whether to
pronounce it cash or cashay, and we didn't trust each other
so much any more. We carried the matchboxes in our
pockets and from time to time—say, at intervals of fifteen
seconds—we opened the matchboxes and bathed in our loot
like the Count of Monte Cristo in the movies. I had little
twinges every now and then, and I'm sure the other kids
did, but we never talked to each other about it, when we
found that the garnets sometimes broke apart when the
knife blade hit them instead of the surrounding sandstone.
I believe I even had a theory that they dried out, hardened,
when exposed to air, because how could they be jewels in
a brooch or a pin or a ring if they broke. Jewels were things
that were very hard. But I didn't worry about it long. There
was some man on the block, not a parent, maybe a furnace
man or a yard man or a handy man or a chauffeur, who was
the court of last resort. He was a grownup, but he leveled

with kids. The day we had found some bullets on the vacant lot, we brought them to him and he put them in a vise and rigged a pin and string up some way and they were real bullets all right. He was not the furnace man, I know that; the furnace man came on a racing bike, without brakes, and we daily cut ourselves into two complete halves riding it, the saddle thin and unpadded and sharp as any knife.

We took the garnets to this man who was on our side: he pronounced them garnets. We went back and split more tons of sandstone. I don't know who it was who finally told us—maybe this same man. They were the kind of garnets used to make that rough sandpaper called garnet paper. They were not jewels at all.

We gave up the magic lantern and the hunting knife with scabbard and hip boots; we waved goodby to the order, no futzing around now, of the entire contents of the Johnson Smith catalog, all in one swoop; we knew we would never have the complete works of Tom Swift. We went back to taking cod-liver oil and being hunted off to bed.

As I write this now, I wonder, is it possible they were real garnets? Would it be worth tearing down the house that sits on that corner and making it into a vacant lot again? Were the rocks hauled off somewhere, and do they sit now on a vacant lot? Anyone for a garnet mine?

The chestnuts are still around. These were horse chestnuts, and next to clothesline, the most useful thing in the world.

When I started my love affair with horse chestnuts, just the way there was only The Reservoir, just one in the world, so there was only one Horse Chestnut Tree.

To get to it, I went out the back door of my house, across the backyard, to the stone wall. Our house was at the bottom of a hill, and the yard that abutted ours was, say, six feet higher than ours. There were a number of footholds in the stone wall, and the age of which I am writing now, there was one that got me to the top of the wall in one climbing step, my belly on the top of the wall, and a certain amount of minor scrabbling with one suspended foot, a certain amount of wriggling, and I was on all fours in the next backyard. I straightened up slowly, and viewed the terrain. For the moment, I was safe, because this was our own stone wall I was standing on. From there on out it was no man's land. There was, after a sortie across the backyard on the right, a driveway. There was, after an even longer expedition across the backyard directly ahead, a path that led from their back door along the side of the house to their front door and thence to the street. I didn't know either of these families. All that meant was that they didn't have kids my age, and consequently they didn't exist.

The driveway to the right was safer, except that that backyard had a flower garden in it, and the lady of the house liked her flower garden. On the other hand, the drive-way was a little ways away from the house. The path directly ahead was right next to its house, therefore right next to people. More than that, there was an unwritten law about cutting through lots. Short cuts were, basically, against The Law. By usage, anyone who objected to your cutting through a driveway was an old grouch, but people who objected to your strolling along their path had a good deal of sweet reason on their side.

The problem was solved one way or another, usually by one kid going one way, one the other, to halve the odds.

It now occurs to me as curious that we should have all this regard for law and order when what we were going to do next was illegal, both by unwritten law, possibly by statute law, and certainly in most vigorous terms by who-ever owned the house that the path led by.

Because on that house's front lawn was The Horse Chest-nut Tree. We visited it for weeks in the Fall before it was time, tried to but could not resist pulling the early green burrs off the lower branches. The prickles on the burrs were not yet hard, but splitting the green burrs was mostly a matter of hitting them with stones on the curb, and splitting the nuts along with the burrs.

A little later on, the prickles on the burrs were harder, and sometimes there was a fingernail hold by which you could split the burrs open without hammering them. Then the horse chestnuts were white, or only partially marbled. All this debris we left on the front lawn of this house.

Later still, one day there would be burrs on the ground. This was the day. The burrs were less green, the prickles pricked, enough to hurt, not enough to draw blood. You split the green burr and you saw the brown, marbled, wonderfully shaped nut, glossy but not shiny, made to rub your thumb over. On the other side, the dry woody button. The dullness of this irregular slightly rough patch was perfection. It made the smooth part smoother. All this wonder was cradled in the green burr lined with dead, soft white.

It is hopeless to try to describe perfection. I will try no longer. I will simply state that to me the noblest work of nature is a horse chestnut.

We wore knickerbockers then, and we filled our pockets with horse chestnuts, and when they were full, dumped them into our pants. There was a simple limit to the number of horse chestnuts a kid could want: As many as there were.

We did this collecting, in plain defiance of the law that stated you could not stand on anyone's front yard unless you knew the people on whose front yard you were standing. When it was a stranger's yard, the moment anyone in the house came to a window or door and hollered, you were in duty bound to go away. Until the person disappeared. If crept up on by such an enemy, you were obliged to listen to the jawing, but you were not compelled to allow yourself to be hit.

(116)

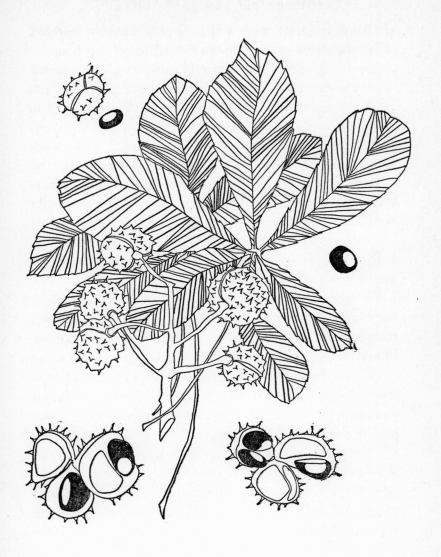

"What did you do?" "NOTHING."

I guess now I know that the people who lived in the house either liked kids or knew that kids were one of the occupational hazards of owning a horse chestnut tree.

The only time they ever hollered, and then not until driven past endurance, was when we, a few days later, would case the tree and find there were no burrs on the ground, but some still on the tree.

We shook the branches, we climbed, but mostly we took sticks and threw them up in the tree to knock the chestnuts loose. We got hit on the head by falling sticks, chestnuts, and each other. They were getting rare now, and we stepped on each other's hands and wrestled some.

All this time, we were sorting out. At that time, I betrayed a character trait which has served me in bad stead all my life. To this day I can walk into a store where they have something I have never bought before: "I should like to see a Sicilian nutmeg soother, if you please." "Why certainly, sir, will you step over here?" There is a tray of Sicilian nutmeg soothers. I look and eventually say, "I think I would like that one in the second row, please." It is a modest enough object. It doesn't have rhinestones, or four-ply driving wheels, like some of the others. The clerk dimples with sheer joy and bridled cupidity. "Oh, you do have good taste, sir. That is our very best, made by Toynbee of Old Franistan Road." All the rest cost three zlotys. This one goes for seventeen hundred cruzeiros.

The same with the chestnuts. The perfect chestnuts were

so perfect, I had to get rid of the ones that had an interrupted marbling here, a pale spot there. Those that were
squirrel- or worm-bitten were immediately out.

Now what did we do with them? Well, first, we just
got them. Then we piled them in piles and were pleased
that we had gotten more than, or better than, our friends.
Then we carried them around in our pockets and showed
them, and traded them, and polished them against the sides
of our noses. We tried to eat them, but could not.

After several weeks of that, we started to use them. They
could be made into pipes, the same as acorns, with straws
for stems. That was for little kids. They could be pierced
with the mumbly-peg blade of a scout knife, strung one at
each end of a string, whirled around the head and caught
on telephone wires. Unlike kites and handkerchief parachutes and model airplanes, this was intentional. This was
the function of this arrangement. I mean, man, these were
made to be caught on telephone wires.

But first, foremost, forever, and I pledge I will teach the
kids on my block this very year, they were meant for the
game of killers.

You take a chestnut, and you hook the ice pick. You wait
until nobody is in the kitchen, and then one kid presses
down on the pilot-light button so that a long delicate blue
finger of flame comes out, and the other kid puts the ice
pick in the flame until it is red-hot. When it is, he bores a
hole in the chestnut. You do as many as you can until some-

body comes and asks you what you are doing, and then, according to your standing in the family, that day, you either plead, argue, or say, "Oh, jeez," and slink away.

In any of these events, the next thing to do is to take the loan of a shoelace. The best kind is the kind that are in your sister's high shoes, and the best way to get it is—well, you know how. If you can't get a shoe lace, heavy brown twine, the kind without the splinters woven in, is okay. A knot in one end, the chestnut strung on, then everybody outside.

You have one. I have one. We choose, odds or evens with fingers. Whoever loses—let's say it's you, for literary ease; you hold up your string with the chestnut dangling. In my right hand I take the end of my string, in my left, the chestnut. I hold the chestnut almost, but not quite, directly above the left hand with string tight and bring it down in a whipping movement. The object, first, is for my chestnut to hit yours, the secondary object is to hit it and break it. This ordinarily does not happen the first time. Now you get a crack at mine.

There is a subsidiary object to this game: if you don't break the other guy's chestnut, but hit it a good one, the string will wrap itself around his fist and with any luck, his chestnut will crack him a good one on the knuckles. It is, however, entirely possible, nay, likely, that if you miss, your chestnut will do that to you.

Sooner or later, a crack will show up in one or both chestnuts. Now an even more delicate *frisson* comes into play:

it is possible that you, striking with a cracked chestnut, will bust yours while hitting at mine. There is a kind of marvelous irony about this that we recognized even then.

We called the chestnuts killers. You had a one-, two-, or forty-killer if you had broken that many chestnuts. However, if a one-killer broke a forty-killer, my memory is that the one-killer became a forty-one-killer, but I am not sure about this.

Other elements of the game were the size of the chestnut: a big one was heavier, obviously, which at first seemed an advantage. But consider: a heavy one hung there, like a dumb beast, and absorbed all punishment. A small one bounced away the moment it was hit. Conversely, when it was time to hit with the small one, you weren't bringing a hell of a lot of weight to bear. It was a toss-up. I owned a small one once, and according to sworn testimony, it was a forty-killer. I liked small ones better.

Skill was of the essence. If you hit it from on top, so that it did not swing like a pendulum, but took the blow, it was odds-on you were going to crack it, but it was also odds-on that if you missed it, you were in for a pretty good knuckle, and you didn't have much chance of getting his knuckle.

As the season went on, the nut itself shrank inside the shell, and the shell was easily cracked, and at the end of the season we were playing not with lovely glossy brown beauties, but with little, gnarled cheesy insides.

Of the folklore of the care and treatment of killers, there

was no end. Roast them like mickies, soak them in Three-in-One oil, store them in the cellar, bury them in talcum powder—but one I remember best. My father, as I have said, was sick. Now we knew, as kids, if a man was very sick, he took very strong medicine. "Jeez, if it's strong medicine for a man, think what it would do to a killer." I took a pinch of this, a wet of that from the medicine chest and dumped it into a milk bottle. I soaked a couple of killers in it.

It was magic. That's how I got my forty-killer. Would that it had been magic for my father.

Well, it's getting on for Fall. I will show the kids about the horse chestnuts.

I keep thinking that they don't know about any of these things, and maybe they don't. But then, grownups when I was a kid didn't know—did they?—any of the world I lived in.

Maybe my kids have got a whole world of their own, with different objects, and I am not admitted to their councils. I devoutly hope so.

My world, as a kid, was full of things that grownups didn't care about. My fear now is that all of us grownups have become so childish that we don't leave the kids much room to move around in, that we foolishly believe that we understand them so well because we share things with them.

This is not only folly, it is not fair. At somebody's house one night, a harassed father who was trying to talk to

"Where did you go?" "OUT."

grownups with his brood around, finally spoke a simple sentence of despair, "For Gossakes, go upstairs or downstairs!"

He was, I believe, asking for privacy. He was, I believe, entitled to it.

I think kids are, too.

Let them moon, let them babble, let them be scared.

I guess what I am saying is that people who don't have nightmares don't have dreams.

If you will excuse me, I have an appointment with myself to sit on the front steps and watch some grass growing.

Spanfeller